For the purpose of offering knowledge, instruction, and encouragement to those who will read and believe, and foremost, to glorify our God.

The Desires of Your Heart
Scriptural Answers to Biblical Questions for youth, new believers, and all who seek to understand!

Published 2015 and 2021 by David Dethrage

Printed by IngramSpark

Photo credit cover: Shutterstock.com
Photo credit church signs: David Dethrage

Book Design: Francine Eden Platt / Eden Graphics, Inc.
edengraphics.net

ISBN print: 978-0-578-91671-2
ISBN ePub: 9781-60645-285-1

SECOND EDITION
Printed in the United States of America

version 6/25/2021

The Desires of Your Heart

SCRIPTURAL ANSWERS *to* BIBLICAL QUESTIONS

For youth, new believers, and all who seek to understand!

Delight in the Lord and he will give you the desires of your heart.

— PSALM 37 : 4 —

Compiled by DAVID DETHRAGE

— Dedication —

This book is lovingly dedicated to my children, Aaron, Stephen, and Carly, God's most perfect and precious gifts to me, and to Kathy Jo Hawkins Dethrage, my former wife for 35 years, for finding God for herself and bringing Him home to us all. Also for this second edition, I add Addison Leigh Baines, my granddaughter, and her father Matthew Baines, as party to the original dedication.

My heart's desire remains family. God has blessed me throughout my life with loving family. From the Huckabys, Watkins, Dethrages, O'Kelleys, Powells, and Cobbs, to the Hawkins, Moons, and Baines, God has so richly Blessed me!
This book is also dedicated to all who have and do call me family!

TABLE OF CONTENTS

Preface

THANK YOU for opening this book. I hope you will find it beneficial. **My greater hope is God will Bless you and God will Bless US.**

This Second Edition of *The Desires of Your Heart* has been published specifically to be given to the members of the United States Congress, the Justices of the United States Supreme Court, Vice President Kamala Harris, and President Joe Biden.

Good Lord willing, I will also include copies to members of the national news media and selected CEOs of America's largest technology companies.

I once hoped the book could be hand-delivered to these individuals by scores of young people as part of a missions project. As I write this Preface I plan to send the book by US Mail.

My son Stephen believes few, if any, of those to whom I mail the book will see, much less take time to consider its contents. I plow on knowing what happens will be in God's hands, and my duty is to plow and plant.

Many think our country is in turmoil and on the brink of destruction. I believe we are at a perilous point in our nation's history, but it is not the first one.

What concerns me most is my belief our nation has lost its moral compass.

Right or wrong, **I think Americans were once confident our government and our intentions were righteous.** Americans believed in the values and principles of our constitution, they trusted our leaders to be God-fearing, and Americans thought **our nation's ambition was to protect and spread freedom and economic opportunity around the globe.**

Something changed. America saw the Kennedys and Dr. King assassinated, prayer was taken from public (government) schools, abortion was legalized, and "political correctness" came to rule the day. During this time America at large was pushing the idea of God's existence, His teachings, and His love further into the background of our nation's psyche.

It seems **our global policy became** less about the well-being of people in other nations and more about **"protecting our national interest."** Frankly, I think my generation, the baby boomers, wallowed around in short-sighted self-fulfillment, greed, and consumerism to the point that we as a nation are indeed in serious trouble.

We find ourselves at odds with one another.

Much of our country's political speech has deteriorated to name-calling and race-baiting.

The national media play with our collective attention span. Their focus seems to draw everything down to politically divisive sides with all attention directed to the next election cycle.

Our nation needs considerate and intelligent debates on the problems, challenges, and opportunities we face.

We need a far greater timeline view than the next election date.

In the coming years let US no longer be known for what divides US.

Let US seek to become known for the love which unites US.

Jesus taught the two greatest commandments are:

Love the Lord your God with all your heart and with all your soul and with all your mind and with all your strength;

AND Love your neighbor as yourself.

Next Jesus told the story of the good Samaritan and thus defined all humans as our "neighbors."

The Creator of the Universe loves us all.

Please, I ask the men and women of the United States Government to **consider God's great love, and I ask for your agreement to work together, love one another, and seek to gain greater knowledge of God's word!**

I pray our nation and our world will come together under the vast umbrella of God's LOVE!

I pray God will Bless you, and Guide you.

I pray you will seek to do as Christ commanded and LOVE!

WITH GOD ALL THINGS ARE POSSIBLE!

I believe there is no problem facing our nation which cannot be solved if our leaders dedicate themselves to love God, love one another, and gain the knowledge and wisdom available in God's word.

David Dethrage 5.11.2021

INTRODUCTION

WHEN I CONSIDER my own salvation, I have serious fear and trembling. I am a lay person and a sinner. If you go looking for means to discredit me, you will not have to look far.

What follows is the result of my effort to teach the words of God at Greenbrier Road Baptist Church in Anniston, Alabama. I taught children, youth, and then adults for six years. Things changed. I no longer teach and I have not been faithful in church attendance. The publication of this book is a personal revival. It is an expression for my love of God and my continuing desire to teach.

I hope you discover this book gets readers quickly "up to speed" on important topics. It provides basic answers to basic Biblical questions. It is a starting point—a road map for discovery. It does not provide all answers to all questions. Hopefully, it will encourage further Bible study.

The answers found here are not mine; there are more than 1,000 Bible verses taken straight from the NIV translation. I have added bold type to highlight the specific answers found within scripture; I have attempted to include enough of the source passages to provide the context in which the answers are written.

I chose to use the NIV Bible because that is the Bible which I believe best "speaks" to me. You should read and study a Bible translation that best speaks to you.

The Word of God is eternal. It instructs, inspires, and enlightens the reader. The Word of God is a historical account of God's relationship with man. It can give us wisdom and lead us to salvation.

The Bible tells us of God's promises. The promise of **Psalm 37:4** is simple: **Delight in the Lord, and He will give you the desires of your heart.** Webster's Dictionary tells us to delight is to "have a high degree of satisfaction" or to "take great pleasure in."

God's love for us is great. He promises to give us those heart-felt desires which matter most **if we will choose to delight in Him.**

I hope this book helps you better understand the Bible and God's awesome love for you. I hope you will be blessed with a stronger appreciation for all God gives us. I hope you will praise God, love all, share His word with others, and most importantly, **DELIGHT in our Lord!**

CALVARY TEMPLE
ASSEMBLY of GOD
GOD LOVES
YOU
SUNDAY MORNING 10:00 WEDNESDAY NIGHT 7:00
REV. JACK LEE, PASTOR

Why was the Bible written?

The Bible was written to give us instruction

Exodus 24:12 The LORD said to Moses, "Come up to me on the mountain and stay here, and I **will give you the tablets of stone, with the law and commandments I have written for their instruction."** 13 Then Moses set out with Joshua his aide, and Moses went up on the mountain of God.

The Bible was written to warn us of the mistakes of others

1 Corinthians 10:1 For I do not want you to be ignorant of the fact, brothers and sisters, that our ancestors were all under the cloud and that they all passed through the sea. 2 They were all baptized into Moses in the cloud and in the sea. 3 They all ate the same spiritual food 4 and drank the same spiritual drink; for they drank from the spiritual rock that accompanied them, and that rock was Christ. 5 Nevertheless, God was not pleased with most of them; their bodies were scattered in the wilderness. 6 **Now these things occurred as examples to keep us from setting our hearts on evil things as they did.** 7 Do not be idolaters, as some of them were; as it is written: "The people sat down to eat and drink and got up to indulge in pagan revelry." 8 We should not commit sexual immorality, as some of them did—and in one day twenty-three thousand of them died. 9 We should not test the Lord, as some of them did—and were killed by snakes. 10 And do not grumble, as some of them did—and were killed by the destroying angel. 11 **These things happened to them as examples and were written down as warnings for us, on whom the culmination of the ages has come.**

The Bible was written to teach us and give us encouragement

Romans 15:1 We who are strong ought to bear with the failings of the weak and not to please ourselves. 2 Each of us should please our neighbors for their good, to build them up. 3 For even Christ did not please himself but, as it is written: "The insults of those who insult you have fallen on me." 4 **For everything that was written in the past was written to teach us, so that through the endurance taught in the Scriptures, and the encouragement they provide, we might have hope.**

The Bible was written to offer assurance

Luke 1:1 Many have undertaken to draw up an account of the things that have been fulfilled among us, 2 just as they were handed down to us by those who from the first were eyewitnesses and servants of the word. 3 With this in mind, since I myself have carefully investigated everything from the beginning, I too decided to write an orderly account for you, most excellent Theophilus, 4 **so that you may know the certainty of the things you have been taught.**

The Bible was written to help us understand Christ

Ephesians 3:1 For this reason I, Paul, the prisoner of Christ Jesus for the sake of you Gentiles— 2 Surely you have heard about the administration of God's grace that was given to me for you, 3 that is, the mystery made known to me by revelation, as I have already written briefly. 4 **In reading this then, you will be able to understand my insight into the mystery of Christ, 5 which was not made known to people in other generations as it has now been revealed by the Spirit to God's holy apostles and prophets.**

Colossians 1:24 Now I rejoice in what I am suffering for you, and I fill up in my flesh what is still lacking in regard to Christ's afflictions, for the sake of his body, which is the church. 25 I have become its servant by **the commission God gave me to present to you the word of God in its fullness— 26 the mystery that has been kept hidden for ages and generations, but is now disclosed to the Lord's people. 27 To them**

God has chosen to make known among the Gentiles the glorious riches of this mystery, which is Christ in you, the hope of glory. [28] He is the one we proclaim, admonishing and teaching everyone with all wisdom, so that we may present everyone fully mature in Christ. [29] To this end I strenuously contend with all the energy of Christ, which so powerfully works in me.

Colossians [2:1] I want you to know how hard I am contending for you and for those at Laodicea, and for all who have not met me personally. [2] **My goal is that they may be encouraged in heart and united in love, so that they may have the full riches of complete understanding, in order that they may know the mystery of God, namely, Christ,** [3] in whom are hidden all the treasures of wisdom and knowledge. [4] I tell you this so that no one may deceive you by fine-sounding arguments. [5] For though I am absent from you in body, I am present with you in spirit and delight to see how disciplined you are and how firm your faith in Christ is.

The Bible was written to stimulate wholesome thinking

2 Peter [3:1] Dear friends, this is now my second letter to you. I have written both of them as reminders **to stimulate you to wholesome thinking.** [2] **I want you to recall the words spoken in the past by the holy prophets and the command given by our Lord and Savior through your apostles.**

The Bible was written to give us blessings

Revelation[1:1] The revelation of Jesus Christ, which God gave him to show his servants what must soon take place. He made it known by sending his angel to his servant John [2] who testifies to everything he saw—that is, the word of God and the testimony of Jesus Christ. [3] **Blessed is the one who reads aloud the words of this prophecy, and blessed are those who hear it and take to heart what is written in it,** because the time is near.

ETERNITY IS A LONG TIME
TO BE WRONG

2 How do we know God really exists?

All mankind knows God

Psalm [19:1] The heavens declare the glory of God; the skies proclaim the work of his hands. [2] Day after day they pour forth speech; night after night they reveal knowledge. [3] They have no speech, they use no words; no sound is heard from them.[4] Yet their voice goes out into all the earth, their words to the ends of the world.

Romans [1:18] The wrath of God is being revealed from heaven against all the godlessness and wickedness of people who suppress the truth by their wickedness, [19] since what may be known about God is plain to them, because God has made it plain to them. [20] **For since the creation of the world God's invisible qualities—his eternal power and divine nature—have been clearly seen, being understood from what has been made, so that people are without excuse.**

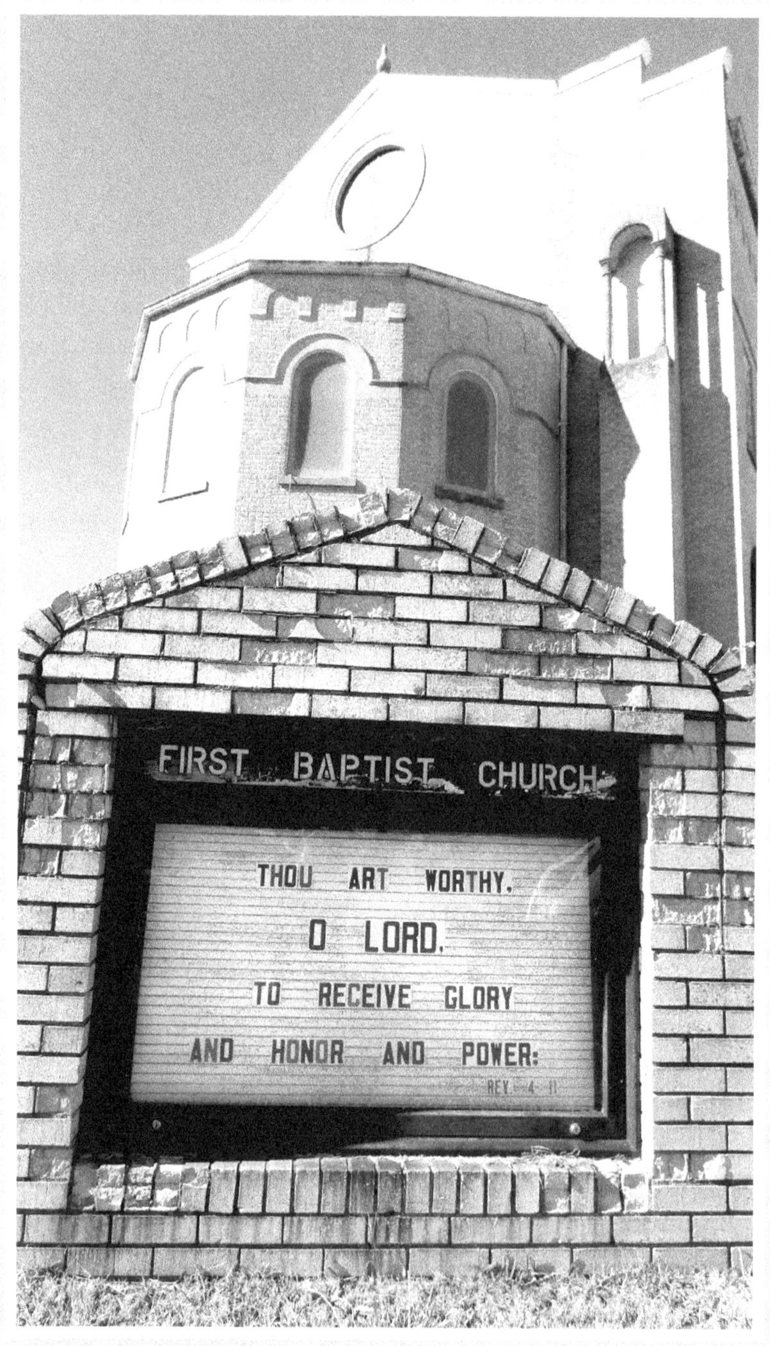
FIRST BAPTIST CHURCH
THOU ART WORTHY,
O LORD,
TO RECEIVE GLORY
AND HONOR AND POWER:
REV. 4 11

Who is God?

God is the Creator

Genesis [1:1] In the beginning **God created the heavens and the earth.**

Genesis [1:27] **So God created mankind** in his own image, in the image of God he created them; male and female he created them.

Psalm [100:3] Know that the LORD is God. **It is he who made us,** and we are his; we are his people, the sheep of his pasture.

1 Samuel [2:6] **The LORD brings death and makes alive;** he brings down to the grave and raises up.

Psalm [33:6] **By the word of the LORD the heavens were made, their starry host by the breath of his mouth.**

Psalm [147:4] **He determines the number of the stars** and calls them each by name.

Proverbs [22:2] Rich and poor have this in common: **The LORD is the Maker of them all.**

God is Mighty

Psalm [93:4] **Mightier than the thunder of the great waters, mightier than the breakers of the sea— the LORD on high is mighty.**

Psalm [147:5] Great is our Lord and **mighty in power;** his understanding has no limit.

God is Loving

Psalm [100:5] For the LORD is good and **his love endures forever;** his faithfulness continues through all generations.

Psalm [103:8] The LORD is compassionate and gracious, slow to anger, **abounding in love.**

Psalm [103:17] But **from everlasting to everlasting the LORD's love is with those who fear him,** and his righteousness with their children's children— [18] with those who keep his covenant and remember to obey his precepts.

Psalm [118:1] Give thanks to the LORD, for he is good; **his love endures forever.**

Psalm [130:7] Israel, put your hope in the LORD, for **with the LORD is unfailing love** and with him is full redemption.

Psalm [145:8] The LORD is gracious and compassionate, slow to anger **and rich in love.**

Psalm [145:9] The LORD is good to all; **he has compassion on all he has made.**

God is Our Strength and Salvation

Exodus [15:2] **The LORD is my strength and my defense; he has become my salvation.**

Psalm [34:22] The LORD will rescue his servants; **no one who takes refuge in him will be condemned.**

God is a Warrior

Exodus [15:3] **The LORD is a warrior; the LORD is his name.**

God is Everywhere

Numbers [14:20] The LORD replied, "I have forgiven them, as you asked. [21] Nevertheless, as surely as I live and as surely as **the glory of the LORD fills the whole earth . . .**"

Psalm [33:5] The LORD loves righteousness and justice; **the earth is full of his unfailing love.**

God is the only God

1 Samuel [2:2] **There is no one holy like the LORD; there is no one besides you; there is no Rock like our God.**

Deuteronomy [4:39] **Acknowledge and take to heart this day that the LORD is God in heaven above and on the earth below. There is no other.** [40] Keep his decrees and commands, which I am giving you today, so that it may go well with you and your children after you and that you may live long in the land the LORD your God gives you for all time.

Jeremiah [10:10] But **the LORD is the true God;** he is the living God, the eternal King. When he is angry, the earth trembles; the nations cannot endure his wrath.

God is King

Psalm [10:16] **The LORD is King for ever and ever;** the nations will perish from his land.

Psalm [93:1] **The LORD reigns, he is robed in majesty;** the LORD is robed in majesty and armed with strength; indeed, the world is established, firm and secure.

Psalm [103:19] **The LORD has established his throne in heaven, and his kingdom rules over all.**

Isaiah [33:22] For the LORD is our judge, the LORD is our lawgiver, **the LORD is our king;** it is he who will save us.

Jeremiah [10:10] But the LORD is the true God; he is the living God, **the eternal King.** When he is angry, the earth trembles; the nations cannot endure his wrath.

God is Judge and Punisher

1 Samuel [2:9] He will guard the feet of his faithful servants, **but the wicked will be silenced in the place of darkness. It is not by strength that one prevails;** [10] those who oppose the LORD will be broken. The Most High will thunder from heaven; **the LORD will judge the ends of the earth.**

Numbers **14:18** The LORD is slow to anger, abounding in love and forgiving sin and rebellion. Yet **he does not leave the guilty unpunished; he punishes the children for the sin of the parents to the third and fourth generation.**

Psalm **9:8** **He will judge the world** in righteousness; and judges the peoples with equity.

Psalm **11:6** **On the wicked he will rain fiery coals and burning sulfur; a scorching wind will be their lot.**

Psalm 34:16 but the face of **the LORD is against those who do evil,** to blot out their name from the earth.

Psalm 145:20 The LORD watches over all who love him, but **all the wicked he will destroy.**

Jeremiah 51:56 A destroyer will come against Babylon; her warriors will be captured, and their bows will be broken. **For the LORD is a God of retribution; he will repay in full.**

Nahum 1:2 The LORD is a jealous and avenging God; the LORD takes vengeance and is filled with wrath. **The LORD takes vengeance on his foes and vents his wrath against his enemies.**

Nahum 1:3 The LORD is slow to anger but great in power; **the LORD will not leave the guilty unpunished.**

New Fellowship
BAPTIST CHURCH
Sunday School 10:00 AM
Worship 11:00 AM
Evening 6:00 PM
Wednesday 6:30 PM
IPOD? IPAD?
TRY IPRAY.
GOD IS LISTENING.

CHEAHA
BAPTIST CHURCH
MAN DOES NOT SEE WHAT
THE LORD SEES - FOR MAN
SEES WHAT IS VISIBLE
SUNDAYSCHOOL
9:00AM
WORSHIP
10:00AM & 6:00PM
STEVEN JOHNSON
PASTOR

4 WHAT ARE GOD'S CHARACTERISTICS?

God has always been

Genesis [1:1] **In the beginning God created the heavens and the earth.**

God knows everything

1 Samuel [2:3] Do not keep talking so proudly or let your mouth speak such arrogance, for **the LORD is a God who knows, and by him deeds are weighed.**

God controls everything

1 Samuel [2:7] **The LORD sends poverty and wealth; he humbles and he exalts.** [8] **He raises the poor from the dust and lifts the needy from the ash heap; he seats them with princes and has them inherit a throne of honor. "For the foundations of the earth are the LORD's; upon them he has set the world."**

God is our protection

1 Samuel [2:9] **He will guard the feet of his faithful servants,** but the wicked will be silenced in the place of darkness.

2 Samuel [22:31] As for God, his way is perfect; the LORD's word is flawless; **he shields all who take refuge in him.**

Psalm [9:9] **The LORD is a refuge for the oppressed, a stronghold in times of trouble.**

Psalm [27:1] **The LORD is my light and my salvation—whom shall I fear? The LORD is the stronghold of my life— of whom shall I be afraid?**

Psalm [34:7] **The angel of the LORD encamps around those who fear him, and he delivers them.**

God brings light

2 Samuel [22:29] **You, LORD, are my lamp; the LORD turns my darkness into light.**

Psalm [19:8] The precepts of the LORD are right, giving joy to the heart. **The commands of the LORD are radiant, giving light to the eyes.**

God is perfect

2 Samuel [22:31] **As for God, his way is perfect; the LORD's word is flawless.**

God is eternal

Psalm [9:7] **The LORD reigns forever;** he has established his throne for judgment.

Psalm [33:11] But **the plans of the LORD stand firm forever,** the purposes of his heart through all generations.

Psalm [93:2] Your throne was established long ago; **you are from all eternity.**

Psalm [100:5] For the LORD is good and **his love endures forever;** his faithfulness continues through all generations.

Psalm [146:10] **The LORD reigns forever,** your God, O Zion, for all generations.

Isaiah [26:4] Trust in the LORD forever, for the LORD, **the LORD himself, is the Rock eternal.**

2 Peter [3:8] But do not forget this one thing, dear friends: **With the Lord a day is like a thousand years, and a thousand years are like a day.**

God waits for our call

2 Chronicles [15:1] The Spirit of God came on Azariah son of Oded. [2] He went out to meet Asa and said to him, "Listen to me, Asa and all Judah and Benjamin. **The LORD is with you when you are with him. If you seek him, he will be found by you, but if you forsake him, he will forsake you."**

Psalm [145:18] **The LORD is near to all who call on him, to all who call on him in truth.**

Jeremiah [33:2] This is what the LORD says, he who made the earth, the LORD who formed it and established it—the LORD is his name: [3] **"Call to me and I will answer you and tell you great and unsearchable things you do not know."**

Malachi [3:7] "Ever since the time of your ancestors you have turned away from my decrees and have not kept them. **Return to me, and I will return to you," says the LORD Almighty.**

God is faithful

Psalm [100:5] For the LORD is good and his love endures forever; **his faithfulness continues through all generations.**

Psalm [9:10] Those who know your name trust in you, **for you, LORD, have never forsaken those who seek you.**

Psalm [145:13] Your kingdom is an everlasting kingdom, and your dominion endures through all generations. **The LORD is trustworthy in all his promises and faithful in all he does.**

2 Thessalonians [3:3] **But the Lord is faithful,** and he will strengthen you and protect you from the evil one.

God watches us

Psalm [11:4] The LORD is in his holy temple; the LORD is on his heavenly throne. **He observes everyone on earth; his eyes examine them.**

Psalm [33:13] From heaven the LORD looks down and **sees all mankind;**

Psalm [33:14] from his dwelling place **he watches all who live on earth—**

Psalm [33:15] he who forms the hearts of all, **who considers everything they do.**

Psalm [33:18] But **the eyes of the LORD are on those who fear him,** on those whose hope is in his unfailing love, [19] to deliver them from death and keep them alive in famine.

Psalm [121:8] **the LORD will watch over your coming and going both now and forevermore.**

Psalm[145:20] **The LORD watches over all who love him,** but all the wicked he will destroy.

God is just

Psalm [9:8] He rules the world in righteousness **and judges the peoples with equity.**

Psalm [11:7] For the LORD is righteous, **he loves justice;** the upright will see his face.

God's word is perfect

2 Samuel [22:31] "As for God, his way is perfect; **the LORD's word is flawless.**

Psalm [12:6] **And the words of the LORD are flawless,** like silver purified in a crucible, like gold refined seven times.

Psalm [18:30] As for God, his way is perfect; **the LORD's word is flawless;** he shields all who take refuge in him.

Psalm [33:4] For the word of **the LORD is right and true;** he is faithful in all he does.

1 Peter [1:24] For, "All people are like grass, and all their glory is like the flowers of the field; the grass withers and the flowers fall, [25] **but the word of the Lord endures forever."**

God hears us

Psalm [34:15] The eyes of the LORD are on the righteous and **his ears are attentive to their cry;**

Psalm [34:17] The righteous cry out, and **the LORD hears them;** he delivers them from all their troubles.

Psalm [145:19] He fulfills the desires of those who fear him; **he hears their cry** and saves them.

God forgives us

Numbers [14:18] **The LORD is slow to anger, abounding in love and forgiving sin and rebellion.** Yet he does not leave the guilty unpunished; he punishes the children for the sin of the parents to the third and fourth generation.

Psalm [103:9] He will not always accuse, nor will he harbor his anger forever; [10] he does not treat us as our sins deserve or repay us according to
our iniquities. [11] For as high as the heavens are above the earth, so great
is his love for those who fear him; [12] **as far as the east is from the west,
so far has he removed our transgressions from us.** [13] As a father has
compassion on his children, so the LORD has compassion on those
who fear him.

God does not sleep

Psalm [121:3] He will not let your foot slip—**he who watches over you will not slumber.**

God knows our mind and our heart

Jeremiah [20:12] LORD Almighty, **you who examine the righteous and probe the heart and mind...**

God does not change

Malachi [3:6] **I the LORD do not change.**

NEW BETHEL
BAPTIST CHURCH

A BIBLE THAT IS
FALLING APART
USUALLY BELONGS TO
SOMEONE WHO ISN'T

Sunday School
10:00 am
Sunday
Morning Worship
11:00 am
Evening Worship
5:30 pm
Wednesday
Bible Study
5:30 pm
Pastor:

5 CAN WE UNDERSTAND GOD?

God is incomprehensible

Psalm 145:3 Great is the LORD and most worthy of praise; **his greatness no one can fathom.**

Judges 13:17 Then Manoah inquired of the angel of the LORD, "What is your name, so that we may honor you when your word comes true?" **18** He replied, **"Why do you ask my name? It is beyond understanding."**

An answer from Job

Job 36:26 How great is God—**beyond our understanding! The number of his years is past finding out.**

Job 37:5 God's voice thunders in marvelous ways; **he does great things beyond our understanding.**

Job 37:23 The Almighty is **beyond our reach** and exalted in power; in his justice and great righteousness, he does not oppress.

Paul wrote even God's love is beyond understanding

Ephesians 3:17 so that Christ may dwell in your hearts through faith. And I pray that you, being rooted and established in love, **18** may have **power, together with all the LORD's holy people, to grasp how wide and long and high and deep is the love of Christ, 19 and to know this love that surpasses knowledge**—that you may be filled to the measure of all the fullness of God.

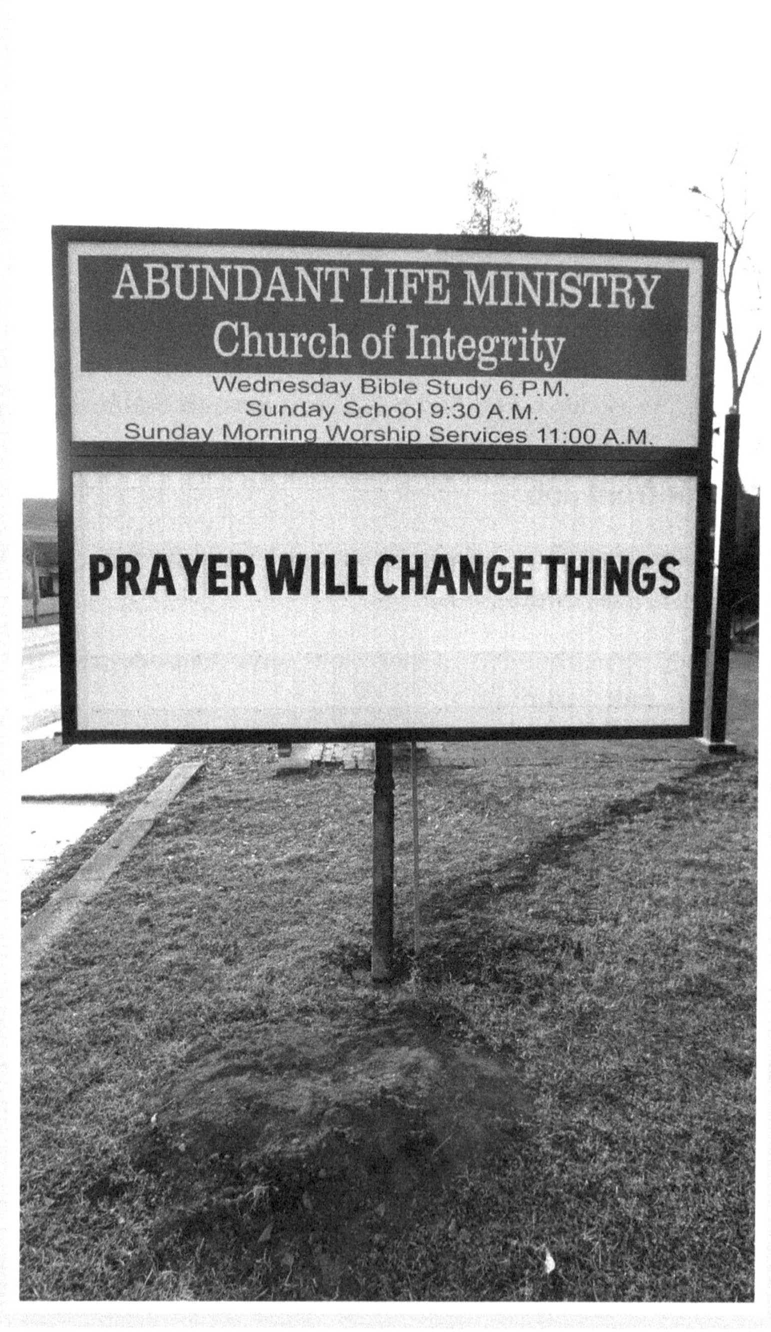
ABUNDANT LIFE MINISTRY
Church of Integrity
Wednesday Bible Study 6.P.M.
Sunday School 9:30 A.M.
Sunday Morning Worship Services 11:00 A.M.
PRAYER WILL CHANGE THINGS

6 What is God Able to Do?

God's knowledge is supreme

Psalm 147:5 Great is our Lord and mighty in power; his understanding has no limit.

There is no "chance" in God's creation

Proverbs 16:33 The lot is cast into the lap, but its **every decision is from the LORD.**

God declares himself to be without equal

Isaiah 40:25 "To whom will you compare me? **Or who is my equal?"** says the Holy One. 26 "Lift up your eyes and look to the heavens: Who created all these? He who brings out the starry host one by one, and calls forth each of them by name. Because of his great power and mighty strength, not one of them is missing. 27 Why do you complain, Jacob, why do you say, Israel, 'My way is hidden from the LORD; my cause is disregarded by my God?' 28 Do you not know? Have you not heard? **The LORD is the everlasting God, the Creator of the ends of the earth. He will not grow tired or weary, and his understanding no one can fathom."**

Paul reminds us God is able to do even more than we can imagine

Ephesians 3:20 Now to him who is **able to do immeasurably more than all we ask or imagine**, according to his power that is at work within us, 21 to him be glory in the church and in Christ Jesus throughout all generations, forever and ever! Amen.

Railroad Avenue
Baptist Church
COME TO MY
HOUSE SUNDAY
BRING THE KIDS
GOD
Pastor
Ricky Maroney
Co-Pastor
Brian Maroney
Sunday School 10:00
Morning Worship 11:00
Evening Worship 5:00
Wednesday Service
Bible Study 6:00

WHAT ARE THE TEN COMMANDMENTS?

The First Four Commandments deal with our relationship with God

Exodus 20:1 And God spoke all these words:

(1) **Exodus** 20:2 "I am the LORD your God, who brought you out of Egypt, out of the land of slavery. 3 **You shall have no other gods before me.**"

(2) **Exodus** 20:4 "**You shall not make for yourself an image** in the form of anything in heaven above or on the earth beneath or in the waters below. 5 You shall not bow down to them or worship them; for I, the LORD your God, am a jealous God, punishing the children for the sin of the parents to the third and fourth generation of those who hate me, 6 but showing love to a thousand generations of those who love me and keep my commandments."

(3) **Exodus** 20:7 "You **shall not misuse the name of the LORD your God**, for the LORD will not hold anyone guiltless who misuses his name."

(4) **Exodus** 20:8 "**Remember the Sabbath day by keeping it holy.** 9 Six days you shall labor and do all your work, 10 but the seventh day is a Sabbath to the LORD your God. On it you shall not do any work, neither you, nor your son or daughter, nor your male or female servant, nor your animals, nor any foreigner residing in your towns. 11 For in six days the LORD made the heavens and the earth, the sea, and all that is in them, but he rested on the seventh day. Therefore the LORD blessed the Sabbath day and made it holy."

The Fifth Commandment concerns our relationship with our parents and includes a promise

(5) **Exodus** 20:12 **"Honor your father and your mother**, so that you may live long in the land the LORD your God is giving you."

The Final Five Commandments concern our relationships with others

(6) **Exodus** 20:13 "You **shall not murder**."

(7) **Exodus** 20:14 "You **shall not commit adultery**."

(8) **Exodus** 20:15 "You **shall not steal.**"

(9) **Exodus** 20:16 "You **shall not give false testimony against your neighbor.**"

(10) **Exodus** 20:17 "You **shall not covet** your neighbor's house. You shall not covet your neighbor's wife, or his male or female servant, his ox or donkey, or anything that belongs to your neighbor."

Sweet Rock
Full Gospel Baptist Church
IS PRAYER YOUR
STEERING WHEEL
OR SPARE TIRE
REV. H. ROGERS MALONE
PASTOR

Fairview
Baptist Church
LIVE BY FAITH,
NOT BY FEAR!
— Pastor —
Bro. Gary Williams
SUNDAY SERVICES
SUNDAY SCHOOL 9:45
MORNING WORSHIP 11:00
DISCIPLESHIP TRAINING 5:00
EVENING WORSHIP 6:00
WEDNESDAY SERVICES
6:00pm
1 MILE
STOP

8 What does God say about the display of the Commandments?

God desires us to never forget his Law

Deuteronomy 6:4 Hear, O Israel: The LORD our God, the LORD is one. 5 Love the LORD your God with all your heart and with all your soul and with all your strength. 6 **These commandments that I give you today are to be on your hearts. 7 Impress them on your children. Talk about them when you sit at home and when you walk along the road, when you lie down and when you get up. 8 Tie them as symbols on your hands and bind them on your foreheads. 9 Write them on the door frames of your houses and on your gates.**

Deuteronomy 11:16 Be careful, or you will be enticed to turn away and worship other gods and bow down to them. 17 Then the LORD's anger will burn against you, and he will shut up the heavens so that it will not rain and the ground will yield no produce, and you will soon perish from the good land the LORD is giving you. 18 **Fix these words of mine in your hearts and minds; tie them as symbols on your hands and bind them on your foreheads. 19 Teach them to your children, talking about them when you sit at home and when you walk along the road, when you lie down and when you get up. 20 Write them on the doorframes of your houses and on your gates, 21 so that your days and the days of your children may be many in the land the LORD swore to give your ancestors, as many as the days that the heavens are above the earth.**

CAST YOUR
CARES ON GOD
FOR HE CARES
FOR YOU
OAK BOWERY
BAPTIST CHURCH

9 Where is God when I need Him most?

God is always with us

Deuteronomy 31:1 Then Moses went out and spoke these words to all Israel: 2 "I am now a hundred and twenty years old and I am no longer able to lead you. The LORD has said to me, 'You shall not cross the Jordan.' 3 The LORD your God himself will cross over ahead of you. He will destroy these nations before you, and you will take possession of their land. Joshua also will cross over ahead of you, as the LORD said. 4 And the LORD will do to them what he did to Sihon and Og, the kings of the Amorites, whom he destroyed along with their land. 5 The LORD will deliver them to you, and you must do to them all that I have commanded you. 6 Be strong and courageous. Do not be afraid or terrified because of them, for **the LORD your God goes with you; he will never leave you nor forsake you."**

Deuteronomy 31:7 Then Moses summoned Joshua and said to him in the presence of all Israel, "Be strong and courageous, for you must go with this people into the land that the LORD swore to their ancestors to give them, and you must divide it among them as their inheritance. 8 **The LORD himself goes before you and will be with you; he will never leave you nor forsake you. Do not be afraid; do not be discouraged."**

God is always ready to help

Psalm 46:1 **God is our refuge and strength, an ever-present help in trouble.** 2 Therefore we will not fear, though the earth give way and the mountains fall into the heart of the sea, 3 though its waters roar and foam and the mountains quake with their surging.

God is with you and will delight in you

Zephaniah [3:17] **The LORD your God is with you, the mighty warrior who saves. He will take great delight in you;** in his love he will no longer rebuke you, but will rejoice over you with singing.

God can be found among the righteous

Psalm [14:5] But there they are, overwhelmed with dread, for **God is present in the company of the righteous.**

Matthew[18:19] Again, truly I tell you that if two of you on earth agree about anything they ask for, it will be done for them by my Father in heaven. [20] For **where two or three gather in my name, there am I with them.**

Jesus is with us and God is with us

Matthew [28:16] Then the eleven disciples went to Galilee, to the mountain where Jesus had told them to go. [17] When they saw him, they worshiped him; but some doubted. [18] Then Jesus came to them and said, "All authority in heaven and on earth has been given to me. [19] Therefore go and make disciples of all nations, baptizing them in the name of the Father and of the Son and of the Holy Spirit, [20] and teaching them to obey everything I have commanded you. And surely **I am with you always, to the very end of the age."**

Luke [17:20] Once, on being asked by the Pharisees when the kingdom of God would come, Jesus replied, "The coming of the kingdom of God is not something that can be observed, [21] nor will people say, 'Here it is,' or 'There it is,' because **the kingdom of God is in your midst."**

God is present in this life and through eternity

Psalm [23:1] The LORD is my shepherd, I lack nothing.

[2] He makes me lie down in green pastures,

[3] he leads me beside quiet waters, he refreshes my soul. He guides me along the right paths for his name's sake.

4 **Even though I walk through the darkest valley, I will fear no evil, for you are with me**; your rod and your staff, they comfort me.

5 You prepare a table before me in the presence of my enemies. You anoint my head with oil; my cup overflows.

6 Surely your goodness and love will follow me all the days of my life, and **I will dwell in the house of the LORD forever.**

PIEDMONT
CHURCH of CHRIST
CAN YOUR LIFE
STAND AN
ETERNAL
AUDIT?

10 Who or What Does the Lord Despise?

God will not tolerate some

Psalm [5:4] For you are not a God who is pleased with wickedness; **with you evil people are not welcome.**

Psalm [5:5] The arrogant cannot stand in your presence; **you hate all who do wrong.**

Psalm [5:6] You destroy those who tell lies; **the blood thirsty and deceitful you, LORD detest.**

God despises the ways of the ungodly

Deuteronomy [18:9] When you enter the land the LORD your God is giving you, do not learn to imitate the detestable ways of the nations there. [10] **Let no one be found among you who sacrifices their son or daughter in the fire, who practices divination or sorcery, interprets omens, engages in witchcraft,** [11] **or casts spells, or who is a medium or spiritist or who consults the dead.** [12] **Anyone who does these things is detestable to the LORD.**

God demands correct behavior

Deuteronomy [27:15] **"Cursed is anyone who makes an idol**—a thing detestable to the LORD, the work of skilled hands—and sets it up in secret." Then all the people shall say, "Amen!"

[16] **"Cursed is anyone who dishonors their father or their mother."** Then all the people shall say, "Amen!"

[17] **"Cursed is anyone who moves their neighbor's boundary stone."** Then all the people shall say, "Amen!"

18 "Cursed is anyone who leads the blind astray on the road."

Then all the people shall say, "Amen!"

19 "Cursed is anyone who withholds justice from the foreigner, the fatherless or the widow."

Then all the people shall say, "Amen!"

20 "Cursed is anyone who sleeps with his father's wife, for he dishonors his father's bed."

Then all the people shall say, "Amen!"

21 "Cursed is anyone who has sexual relations with any animal."

Then all the people shall say, "Amen!"

22 "Cursed is anyone who sleeps with his sister, the daughter of his father or the daughter of his mother."

Then all the people shall say, "Amen!"

23 "Cursed is anyone who sleeps with his mother-in-law."

Then all the people shall say, "Amen!"

24 "Cursed is anyone who kills their neighbor secretly."

Then all the people shall say, "Amen!"

25 "Cursed is anyone who accepts a bribe to kill an innocent person."

Then all the people shall say, "Amen!"

26 "Cursed is anyone who does not uphold the words of this law by carrying them out."

Then all the people shall say, "Amen!"

Who the Lord hates

Psalm 11:5 The LORD examines the righteous, but the wicked, those who love violence, he hates with a passion.

Seven things God finds detestable

Proverbs [6:16] There are six things the LORD hates, **seven that are detestable to him:**

(1) [17] **haughty eyes,**

(2) **a lying tongue,**

(3) **hands that shed innocent blood,**

(4) [18] **a heart that devises wicked schemes,**

(5) **feet that are quick to rush into evil,**

(6) [19] **a false witness who pours out lies**

(7) **and a person who stirs up conflict in the community.**

Jesus warns us

Luke [16:13] "No one can serve two masters. Either you will hate the one and love the other, or you will be devoted to the one and despise the other. You cannot serve both God and money." [14] The Pharisees, who loved money, heard all this and were sneering at Jesus. [15] He said to them, "You are the ones who justify yourselves in the eyes of others, but God knows your hearts. **What people value highly is detestable in God's sight."**

Luke [17:1] Jesus said to his disciples: **"Things that cause people to stumble are bound to come, but woe to anyone through whom they come.** [2] It would be better for them to be thrown into the sea with a millstone tied around their neck than to cause one of these little ones to stumble. [3] So watch yourselves."

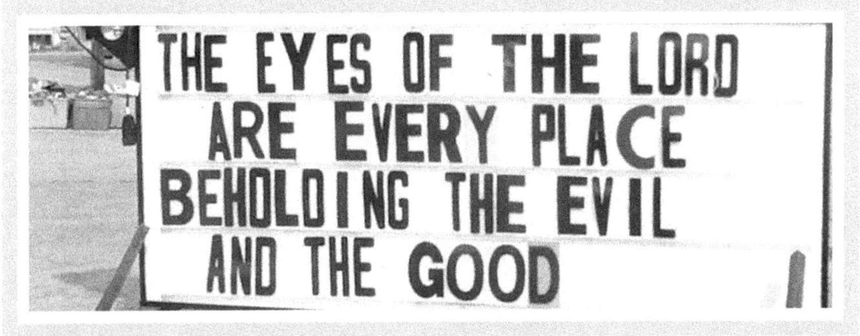

WEAVER
Congregational Holiness
Church
ALWAYS
REMEMBER
THAT HELL
IS UN COOL

Is The Devil Real?

Jesus was tempted by the devil

Matthew [4:1] **Then Jesus was led by the Spirit into the wilderness to be tempted by the devil.** [2] After fasting forty days and forty nights, he was hungry. [3] **The tempter came to him** and said, "If you are the Son of God, tell these stones to become bread."

God talks to Satan

Job [1:6] One day the angels came to present themselves before the LORD, and Satan also came with them. [7] The LORD said to Satan, "Where have you come from?" **Satan answered the LORD, "From roaming throughout the earth going back and forth on it."**

Peter describes the devil

1 Peter [5:8] Be alert and of sober mind. **Your enemy the devil prowls around like a roaring lion looking for someone to devour.** [9] Resist him, standing firm in the faith, because you know that the family of believers throughout the world is undergoing the same kind of sufferings.

The devil is a thief

Luke [8:11] "This is the meaning of the parable: The seed is the word of God. [12] Those along the path are the ones who hear, and then **the devil comes and takes away the word from their hearts, so that they may not believe and be saved.**

Jesus called the devil a murderer and the father of lies

John [8:44] You belong to your father, **the devil,** and you want to carry out your father's desires. **He was a murderer from the beginning, not holding to the truth, for there is no truth in him. When he lies, he speaks his native language, for he is a liar and the father of lies.**

The devil works through man

Luke [22:3] **Then Satan entered Judas**, called Iscariot, one of the Twelve. [4] And Judas went to the chief priests and the officers of the temple guard and discussed with them how he might betray Jesus.

1 John [3:7] Dear children, do not let anyone lead you astray. The one who does what is right is righteous, just as he is righteous. [8] The one who does what is sinful is of the devil, **because the devil has been sinning from the beginning. The reason the Son of God appeared was to destroy the devil's work.** [9] No one who is born of God will continue to sin, because God's seed remains in them; they cannot go on sinning, because they have been born of God. [10] **This is how we know who the children of God are and who the children of the devil are: Anyone who does not do what is right is not God's child, nor is anyone who does not love their brother and sister.**

Envy and selfish ambition are of the devil

James [3:13] Who is wise and understanding among you? Let them show it by their good life, by deeds done in the humility that comes from wisdom. [14] But **if you harbor bitter envy and selfish ambition in your hearts, do not boast about it or deny the truth.** [15] **Such "wisdom" does not come down from heaven but is earthly, unspiritual, demonic.** [16] For where you have envy and selfish ambition, there you find disorder and every evil practice.

James tells us we do have hope

James [4:7] Submit yourselves, then, to God. **Resist the devil, and he will flee from you.**

The fate of the devil is known

Matthew[25:41] Then he will say to those on his left, **"Depart from me, you who are cursed, into the eternal fire prepared for the devil and his angels."**

Revelation [20:10] And the devil, who deceived them, was thrown into the lake of burning sulfur, where the beast and the false prophet had been thrown. They will be tormented day and night forever and ever.

Railroad Avenue
Baptist Church
WHATS IN
HELL
THAT YOU WANT

12 Is there a place called Hell?

Jesus teaches of Hell

Matthew [5:29] If your right eye causes you to stumble, gouge it out and throw it away. **It is better for you to lose one part of your body than for your whole body to be thrown into hell.** [30] And if your right hand causes you to stumble, cut it off and throw it away. **It is better for you to lose one part of your body than for your whole body to go into hell.**

Jesus warns us of whom to truly fear

Matthew [10:26] So do not be afraid of them. There is nothing concealed that will not be disclosed, or hidden that will not be made known. [27] What I tell you in the dark, speak in the daylight; what is whispered in your ear, proclaim from the roofs. [28] **Do not be afraid of those who kill the body but cannot kill the soul. Rather, be afraid of the One who can destroy both soul and body in hell.**

A great divide exists between Heaven and Hell

Luke [16:19] There was a rich man who was dressed in purple and fine linen and lived in luxury every day. [20] At his gate was laid a beggar named Lazarus, covered with sores [21] and longing to eat what fell from the rich man's table. Even the dogs came and licked his sores. [22] The time came when the beggar died and the angels carried him to Abraham's side. The rich man also died and was buried. [23] **In Hades, where he was in torment,** he looked up and saw Abraham far away, with Lazarus by his side. [24] So he called to him, "Father Abraham, have pity on me and send Lazarus to dip the tip of his finger in water and cool my tongue, because **I am in agony in this fire.**" [25] "But Abraham replied, "Son, remember that in your lifetime you received your good things, while Lazarus received bad things, but now he is comforted here and you are in agony. [26] And besides all this, **between us and you a great chasm has been set in place, so that those who want to go from here to you cannot, nor can anyone cross over from there to us."**

Church of Christ
at
EASTABOGA
THE DUST RETURN TO
THE EARTH AND THE
SPIRIT RETURNS
TO GOD
SUNDAY SCHOOL: 9:30
MORNING WORSHIP: 10:30
SUNDAY NIGHT: 5:00
WEDNESDAY NIGHT: 7:00

13 What Will Happen on Judgment Day?

God will judge all mankind

Psalm 9:7 The LORD reigns forever; **he has established his throne for judgment.**

Ecclesiastes 11:9 You who are young, be happy while you are young, and let your heart give you joy in the days of your youth. Follow the ways of your heart and whatever your eyes see, but know that for all these things **God will bring you into judgment.**

Romans 14:9 For this very reason, Christ died and returned to life so that he might be the Lord of both the dead and the living. 10 You, then, why do you judge your brother or sister? Or why do you treat them with contempt? For **we will all stand before God's judgment seat.** 11 It is written: "As surely as I live," says the Lord, "every knee will bow before me; every tongue will acknowledge God." 12 **So then, each of us will give an account of ourselves to God.**

Hebrews 4:12 For the word of God is alive and active. Sharper than any double-edged sword, it penetrates even to dividing soul and spirit, joints and marrow; it judges the thoughts and attitudes of the heart. 13 Nothing in all creation is hidden from God's sight. **Everything is uncovered and laid bare before the eyes of him to whom we must give account.**

Hebrews 9:27 Just as people are **destined to die once, and after that to face judgment,** 28 so Christ was sacrificed once to take away the sins of many; and he will appear a second time, not to bear sin, but to bring salvation to those who are waiting for him.

2 Corinthians 5:6 Therefore we are always confident and know that as long as we are at home in the body we are away from the Lord. 7 For we live by faith, not by sight. 8 We are confident, I say, and would prefer to be away from the body and at home with the Lord. 9 So we make it our goal to please him, whether we are at home in the body or away from it. 10 **For we must all appear before the judgment seat of Christ, that each one may receive what is due us for the things done while in the body, whether good or bad.**

1 Timothy 5:24 **The sins of some are obvious, reaching the place of judgment ahead of them**; the sins of others trail behind them. 25 In the same way, good deeds are obvious, and even those that are not obvious can not remain hidden forever.

Hebrews 10:26 If we deliberately keep on sinning after we have received the knowledge of the truth, no sacrifice for sins is left, 27 but only **a fearful expectation of judgment and of raging fire that will consume the enemies of God.** 28 Anyone who rejected the law of Moses died without mercy on the testimony of two or three witnesses. 29 How much more severely do you think someone deserves to be punished who has trampled the Son of God under foot, who has treated as an unholy thing the blood of the covenant that sanctified them, and who has insulted the Spirit of grace? 30 For we know him who said, "It is mine to avenge; I will repay," and again, **"The Lord will judge his people." 31 It is a dreadful thing to fall into the hands of the living God.**

Revelation 20:11 Then I saw a great white throne and him who was seated on it. The Earth and the heavens fled from his presence, and there was no place for them. 12 And I saw the dead, great and small, standing before the throne, and books were opened. Another book was opened, which is the book of life. The dead were judged according to what they had done as recorded in the books. 13 The sea gave up the dead that were in it, and death and Hades gave up the dead that were in them, and each person was judged according to what they had done. 14 Then death and Hades were thrown into the lake of fire. The lake of fire is the second death. 15 Anyone whose name was not found written in the book of life was thrown into the lake of fire.

Our life and our actions matter

Matthew 12:33 “Make a tree good and its fruit will be good, or make a tree bad and its fruit will be bad, for a tree is recognized by its fruit. 34 You brood of vipers, how can you who are evil say anything good? For the mouth speaks what the heart is full of. 35 A good man brings good things out of the good stored up in him, and an evil man brings evil things out of the evil stored up in him. 36 **But I tell you that everyone will have to give account on the day of judgment for every empty word they have spoken.** 37 For by your words you will be acquitted, and by your words you will be condemned.”

God’s wrath and God’s glory will be seen

Romans 2:5 But because of your stubbornness and your unrepentant heart, **you are storing up wrath against yourself for the day of God’s wrath, when his righteous judgment will be revealed.** 6 God “will repay each person according to what they have done.” 7 To those who by persistence in doing good seek glory, honor and immortality, he will give eternal life. 8 But **for those who are self-seeking and who reject the truth and follow evil, there will be wrath and anger**. 9 There will be trouble and distress for every human being who does evil: first for the Jew, then for the Gentile; 10 **but glory, honor and peace for everyone who does good:** first for the Jew, then for the Gentile. 11 For God does not show favoritism.

2 Peter 3:3 Above all, you must understand that in the last days scoffers will come, scoffing and following their own evil desires. 4 They will say, “Where is this ‘coming’ he promised? Ever since our ancestors died, everything goes on as it has since the beginning of creation.” 5 But they deliberately forget that long ago by God’s word the heavens came into being and the earth was formed out of water and by water. 6 By these waters also the world of that time was deluged and destroyed. 7 **By the same word the present heavens and earth are reserved for fire, being kept for the day of judgment and destruction of the ungodly.**

We can have confidence in God's love

1 John 4:13 This is how we know that we live in him and he in us; He has given us of his Spirit. 14 And we have seen and testify that the Father has sent his Son to be the Savior of the world. 15 If anyone acknowledges that Jesus is the Son of God, God lives in them and they in God. 16 **And so we know and rely on the love God has for us. God is love. Whoever lives in love lives in God, and God in them.** 17 **This is how love is made complete among us so that we will have confidence on the day of judgment; In this world we are like Jesus.** 18 There is no fear in love. But perfect love drives out fear, because fear has to do with punishment. The one who fears is not made perfect in love.

MT. PISGAH
BAPTIST CHURCH
CHOICE
NOT CHANCE
DETERMINES
YOUR DESTINY
Sunday School
9:45
Worship Service
11:00 & 5:00

ABUNDANT LIFE MINISTRY
Church of Integrity
Wednesday Bible Study 6.P.M.
Sunday School 9:30 A.M.
Sunday Morning Worship Services 11:00 A.M.
DONT WORRY GOD
WILL ALWAYS
MAKE A WAY
Jeffery Leonard
Pastor
Doris Leonard
Minister

14 What is the Mark of The Beast?

In the end times a great power will rise up and control the world

Revelation 13:5 **The beast** was given a mouth to utter proud words and blasphemies and to exercise its authority for forty-two months. 6 It opened its mouth to blaspheme God, and to slander his name and his dwelling place and those who live in heaven. 7 It **was given power to wage war against God's holy people and to conquer them. And it was given authority over every tribe, people, language and nation.** 8 All inhabitants of the earth will worship the beast—all whose names have not been written in the Lamb's book of life—the Lamb who was slain from the creation of the world.

The mark will be a difficult test for Christians

Revelation 13:9 Whoever has ears, let them hear. 10 If anyone is to go into captivity, into captivity they will go. If anyone is to be killed with the sword, with the sword they will be killed. **This calls for patient endurance and faithfulness on the part of God's people.**

Revelation 13:11 Then I saw a second beast, coming out of the earth. It had two horns like a lamb, but it spoke like a dragon. 12 It exercised all the authority of the first beast on its behalf, and made the earth and its inhabitants worship the first beast, whose fatal wound had been healed. 13 And it performed great and miraculous signs, even causing fire to come down from heaven to earth in full view of the people. 14 Because of the signs it was given power to perform on behalf of the first beast, **it deceived the inhabitants of the earth.** It ordered them to set up an image in honor of the beast who was wounded by the sword and yet lived. 15 The second beast was given power to give breath to the image of the first beast, so that the image could speak and **cause all who refused**

to worship the image to be killed. [16] It also forced all people, great and small, rich and poor, free and slave, to receive a mark on their right hands or on their foreheads, [17] so that they could not buy or sell unless they had the mark, which is the name of the beast or the number of its name. **[18]** This calls for wisdom. Let the person who has insight calculate the number of the beast, for it is the number of man. That number is 666.

There will be punishment for those who receive the mark

Revelation [14:9] A third angel followed them and said in a loud voice: **"If anyone worships the beast and its image and receives its mark on their forehead or on their hand, [10] they, too, will drink of the wine of God's fury,** which has been poured full strength into the cup of his wrath. They will be tormented with burning sulfur in the presence of the holy angels and of the Lamb. [11] And the smoke of their torment will rise forever and ever. **There will be no rest day or night for those who worship the beast and its image, or for anyone who receives the mark of its name." [12] This calls for patient endurance on the part of people of God who keep his commandments and remain faithful to Jesus.**

And blessing for those who deny the mark

Revelation [14:13] Then I heard a voice from heaven say, "Write this: **Blessed are the dead who die in the Lord from now on."** Yes," says the Spirit, "they will rest from their labor, for their deeds will follow them."

The mark comes from a false prophet

Revelation [19:19] Then I saw the beast and the kings of the earth and their armies gathered together to wage war against the rider on the horse and his army. [20] But **the beast was captured, and with it the false prophet who had performed the signs on its behalf. With these signs he had deluded those who had received the mark of the beast and worshiped its image.** The two of them were thrown alive into the fiery lake of burning sulfur. [21] The rest were killed with the sword coming out of the mouth of the rider on the horse, and all the birds gorged themselves on their flesh.

Reward for refusing the mark

Revelation 20:4 I saw thrones on which were seated those who had been given authority to judge. And I saw the souls of those who had been beheaded because of their testimony about Jesus and because of the word of God. **They had not worshiped the beast or its image and had not received its mark on their foreheads or their hands. They came to life and reigned with Christ a thousand years.**

Cross Creek
COMMUNITY CHURCH
NEED EXERCISE ?
WALK WITH JESUS
RUN FROM SATAN
SUNDAY SCHOOL
9AM
WORSHIP 10AM
Chris Walker
Pastor

15 Who is Jesus?

Jesus is the Beginning and the End

Revelation 22:12 "Look, I am coming soon! My reward is with me, and I will give to each person according to what they have done. 13 **I am the Alpha and the Omega, the First and the Last, the Beginning and the End.** 14 Blessed are those who wash their robes, that they may have the right to the tree of life and may go through the gates into the city. 15 Outside are the dogs, those who practice magic arts, the sexually immoral, the murderers, the idolaters and everyone who loves and practices falsehood. 16 I, Jesus, have sent my angel to give you this testimony for the churches. I am the Root and the Offspring of David, and the bright Morning Star."

Jesus has been with God since the beginning of time

John 1:1 In the beginning was the Word, and the Word was with God, and the Word was God. 2 **He was with God in the beginning.** 3 Through him all things were made; without him nothing was made that has been made. 4 In him was life, and that life was the light of men.

In Jesus, the Word of God became flesh

John 1:14 **The Word became flesh and made his dwelling among us.** We have seen his glory, the glory of the One and Only, who came from the Father, full of grace and truth.

Jesus was conceived by the Holy Spirit and given his name by an angel

Matthew 1:20 But after he had considered this, **an angel of the Lord** appeared to him in a dream and **said, "Joseph son of David, do not be**

afraid to take Mary home as your wife, because what is conceived in her is from the Holy Spirit. 21 She will give birth to a son, and you are to give him the name Jesus, because he will save his people from their sins."

Jesus is a Miracle Worker

Mark 2:8 Immediately Jesus knew in his spirit that this was what they were thinking in their hearts, and he said to them, "Why are you thinking these things? 9 Which is easier: to say to this paralyzed man, 'Your sins are forgiven,' or to say, 'Get up, take your mat and walk'? 10 But I want you to know that the Son of Man has authority on earth to forgive sins." So he said to the man, 11 "I tell you, get up, take your mat and go home." 12 He got up, took his mat and walked out in full view of them all. **This amazed everyone and they praised God, saying, "We have never seen anything like this!"**

Mark 7:36 Jesus commanded them not to tell anyone. But the more he did so, the more they kept talking about it. 37 **People were overwhelmed with amazement. "He has done everything well," they said. "He even makes the deaf hear and the mute speak."**

Jesus is a Teacher

John 13:12 When he had finished washing their feet, he put on his clothes and returned to his place. "Do you understand what I have done for you?" he asked them. 13 **"You call me 'Teacher' and 'Lord,' and rightly so, for that is what I am.** 14 Now that I, your Lord and Teacher, have washed your feet, you also should wash one another's feet. 15 I have set you an example that you should do as I have done for you. 16 Very truly I tell you, no servant is greater than his master, nor is a messenger greater than the one who sent him. 17 Now that you know these things, you will be blessed if you do them.

Jesus is a Preacher

Mark 1:35 Very early in the morning, while it was still dark, Jesus got up, left the house and went off to a solitary place, where he prayed. 36 Simon and his companions went to look for him, [37] and when they found him, they exclaimed: "Everyone is looking for you!" **[38]** Jesus replied**, "Let us go somewhere else—to the nearby villages—so I can preach there also. That is why I have come."** [39] So he traveled throughout Galilee, preaching in their synagogues and driving out demons.

Jesus is God's Son

Matthew [3:16] As soon as Jesus was baptized, he went up out of the water. At that moment heaven was opened, and he saw the Spirit of God descending like a dove and lighting on him. [17] **And a voice from heaven said, "This is my Son, whom I love; with him I am well pleased."**

Matthew [17:1] After six days Jesus took with him Peter, James and John the brother of James, and led them up a high mountain by themselves. [2] There he was transfigured before them. His face shone like the sun, and his clothes became as white as the light. [3] Just then there appeared before them Moses and Elijah, talking with Jesus. [4] Peter said to Jesus, "Lord, it is good for us to be here. If you wish, I will put up three shelters—one for you, one for Moses and one for Elijah." [5] While he was still speaking, a bright cloud covered them, and a voice from the cloud said, **"This is my Son, whom I love; with him I am well pleased. Listen to him!"**

2 Peter [1:16] We did not follow cleverly devised stories when we told you about the coming of our Lord Jesus Christ in power, but we were eyewitnesses of his majesty. [17] For he received honor and glory from God the Father when the voice came to him from the Majestic Glory, saying, "This is my Son, whom I love; with him I am well pleased." **[18] We ourselves heard this voice that came from heaven** when we were with him on the sacred mountain.

Luke [2:41] Every year Jesus' parents went to Jerusalem for the Feast of the Passover. [42] When he was twelve years old, they went up to the Feast, according to the custom. [43] After the Feast was over, while his parents were returning home, the boy Jesus stayed behind in Jerusalem, but they were unaware of it. [44] Thinking he was in their company, they traveled on for a day. Then they began looking for him among their relatives and friends. [45] When they did not find him, they went back to Jerusalem to look for him. 46 **After three days they found him in the temple courts, sitting among the teachers, listening to them and asking them questions.** 47 **Everyone who heard him was amazed at his understanding and his answers.** 48 When his parents saw him, they were astonished. His mother said to him, "Son, why have you treated us like this? Your father and I have been anxiously searching for you." 49 "Why were you searching for me?" he asked. "**Didn't you know I had to be in my Father's house?**" 50 But they did not understand what he was saying to them. 51 Then he went down to Nazareth with them and was obedient to them. But his mother treasured all these things in her heart. 52 And **Jesus grew in wisdom and stature, and in favor with God and men.**

Jesus led many followers

John 12:17 Now the crowd that was with him when he called Lazarus from the tomb and raised him from the dead continued to spread the word. 18 Many people, because they had heard that he had performed this sign, went out to meet him. 19 **So the Pharisees said to one another, "See, this is getting us nowhere. Look how the whole world has gone after him!"**

Luke 5:15 Yet the news about him spread all the more, so that **crowds of people came to hear him** and to be healed of their sicknesses. 16 But Jesus often withdrew to lonely places and prayed.

Jesus knew his destiny

Luke 18:31 Jesus took the Twelve aside and told them, **"We are going up to Jerusalem, and everything that is written by the prophets about the Son of Man will be fulfilled.** 32 **He will be handed over to the Gentiles. They will mock him, insult him, spit on him; they will flog him and kill him.** 33 **On the third day he will rise again."**

Jesus did not want to be crucified

Matthew 26:36 Then Jesus went with his disciples to a place called Gethsemane, and he said to them, "Sit here while I go over there and pray." 37 He took Peter and the two sons of Zebedee along with him, and he began to be sorrowful and troubled. 38 Then he said to them, **"My soul**

is overwhelmed with sorrow to the point of death. Stay here and keep watch with me."

Matthew 26:39 Going a little farther, he fell with his face to the ground and prayed, **"My Father, if it is possible, may this cup be taken from me. Yet not as I will, but as you will."**

Luke 22:39 Jesus went out as usual to the Mount of Olives, and his disciples followed him. 40 On reaching the place, he said to them, "Pray that you will not fall into temptation." 41 He withdrew about a stone's throw beyond them, knelt down and prayed, 42 **"Father, if you are willing, take this cup from me; yet not my will, but yours be done."** 43 An angel from heaven appeared to him and strengthened him. 44 And being in anguish, he prayed more earnestly, and **his sweat was like drops of blood falling to the ground.**

Jesus offered Himself as a sacrifice to save those who would believe

Mark 10:41 When the ten heard about this, they became indignant with James and John. 42 Jesus called them together and said, "You know that those who are regarded as rulers of the Gentiles lord it over them, and their high officials exercise authority over them. 43 Not so with you. Instead, whoever wants to become great among you must be your servant, 44 and whoever wants to be first must be slave of all. 45 **For even the Son of Man did not come to be served, but to serve, and to give his life as a ransom for many."**

John 3:16 "For God so loved the world that he gave his one and only Son, that **whoever believes in him shall not perish but have eternal life.** 17 For God did not send his Son into the world to condemn the world, but to save the world through him.

Jesus declared Himself to be the Son of God

John 4:21 "Woman," Jesus replied, "a time is coming when you will worship the Father neither on this mountain nor in Jerusalem. 22 You Samaritans worship what you do not know; we worship what we do know, for salvation is from the Jews. 23 Yet a time is coming and has now come when the true worshipers will worship the Father in spirit and truth, for they are the kind of worshipers the Father seeks. [24] God is spirit, and his worshipers must worship in the Spirit and in truth." [25] The woman said, "I know that Messiah (called Christ) is coming. When he comes, he will explain everything to us." [26] Then Jesus declared, **"I, the one speaking to you—I am he."**

Luke [22:66] At daybreak the council of the elders of the people, both the chief priests and teachers of the law, met together, and Jesus was led before them. [67] "If you are the Messiah," they said, "tell us." Jesus answered, "If I tell you, you will not believe me, [68] and if I asked you, you would not answer. [69] But from now on, the Son of Man will be seated at the right hand of the mighty God." [70] **They all asked, "Are you then the Son of God?" He replied, "You say that I am."**

John [10:36] "what about the one whom the Father set apart as his very own and sent into the world? Why then do you accuse me of blasphemy because **I said, 'I am God's Son'**? [37] Do not believe me unless I do the works of my Father. [38] But if I do them, even though you do not believe me, believe the works, that you may know and **understand that the Father is in me, and I in the Father."** [39] Again they tried to seize him, but he escaped their grasp.

On the day of judgment Jesus will acknowledge His own before God and the angels

Matthew [10:28] Do not be afraid of those who kill the body but cannot kill the soul. Rather, be afraid of the One who can destroy both soul and body in hell. [29] Are not two sparrows sold for a penny? Yet not one of them will fall to the ground outside your Father's care. [30] And even the very hairs of your head are all numbered. [31] So don't be afraid; you are worth more than many sparrows. [32] **Whoever acknowledges me before others, I will also acknowledge before my Father in heaven.** [33] But whoever disowns me before others, I will disown before my Father in heaven.

Revelation [3:2] Wake up! Strengthen what remains and is about to die, for I have found your deeds unfinished in the sight of my God. [3] Remember, therefore, what you have received and heard; hold it fast, and repent. But if you do not wake up, I will come like a thief, and you will not know at what time I will come to you. [4] Yet you have a few people in Sardis who have not soiled their clothes. They will walk with me, dressed in white, for they are worthy. [5] **The one who is victorious will, like them, be dressed in white. I will never blot out that person from the book of life, but will acknowledge that name before my Father and his angels.** [6] Whoever has ears, let him hear what the Spirit says to the churches.

Jesus is the path to God

John [14:5] Thomas said to him, "Lord, we don't know where you are going, so how can we know the way?" [6] Jesus answered, "**I am the way and the truth and the life. No one comes to the Father except through me.**

BETTA VIEW HILLS
Church of Christ
SATAN DIVIDES
BUT JESUS UNITES
MINISTER JOHN ROSS

16 In What Way Has Jesus Been Misunderstood?

King Herod thought Jesus to be a reincarnation

Mark [6:14] King Herod heard about this, for Jesus' name had become well known. Some were saying, "John the Baptist has been raised from the dead, and that is why miraculous powers are at work in him." [15] Others said, "He is Elijah." And still others claimed, "He is a prophet, like one of the prophets of long ago." [16] **But when Herod heard this, he said, "John, whom I beheaded, has been raised from the dead!"**

Even some family members said He was crazy

Mark [3:20] Then Jesus entered a house, and again a crowd gathered, so that he and his disciples were not even able to eat. [21] When his family heard about this, they went to take charge of him, for they said, "**He is out of his mind.**"

Jesus was called demon-possessed and a "mere man"

John [10:19] The Jews who heard these words were again divided. [20] **Many of them said, "He is demon-possessed and raving mad.** Why listen to him?" [21] But others said, "These are not the sayings of a man possessed by a demon. Can a demon open the eyes of the blind?"

John [10:31] Again his Jewish opponents picked up stones to stone him, [32] but Jesus said to them, "I have shown you many good works from the Father. For which of these do you stone me?" [33] "We are not stoning you for any good work," replied the Jews, "but for blasphemy, because **you, a mere man, claim to be God.**"

Jesus was laughed at

Mark 5:37 He did not let anyone follow him except Peter, James and John the brother of James. 38 When they came to the home of the synagogue leader, Jesus saw a commotion, with people crying and wailing loudly. 39 He went in and said to them, "Why all this commotion and wailing? The child is not dead but asleep." 40 But **they laughed at him.**

Jesus offended some

Mark 6:1 Jesus left there and went to his hometown, accompanied by his disciples. 2 When the Sabbath came, he began to teach in the synagogue, and many who heard him were amazed. "Where did this man get these things?" they asked. "What's this wisdom that has been given him? What are these remarkable miracles he is performing? 3 Isn't this the carpenter? Isn't this Mary's son and the brother of James, Joseph, Judas and Simon? Aren't his sisters here with us?" **And they took offense at him.**

MIRACLE REVIVAL
TEMPLE
JESUS IS THE
LORD OF LIFE.
IS HE THE
LORD OF YOURS?!

BETHEL MISSIONARY
BAPTIST CHURCH
TGIF
THANK GOD
I'M FORGIVEN
SUNDAY SCHOOL 9:30 MORNING WORSHIP 10:45
WEDNESDAY MEETING 6:00

Who were the Disciples?

There were twelve disciples

Matthew 10:1 Jesus called his twelve disciples to him and gave them authority to drive out impure spirits and to heal every disease and sickness.

2 These are the names of the twelve apostles:
first, **Simon** (who is called Peter) and
his brother **Andrew**;
James son of Zebedee, and
his brother **John**;
3 **Philip** and
Bartholomew;
Thomas and
Matthew the tax collector;
James son of Alphaeus, and
Thaddaeus;
4 **Simon the Zealot** and
Judas Iscariot, who betrayed him.

After Judas' betrayal a replacement was chosen

Acts 1:21 Therefore it is necessary to choose one of the men who have
been with us the whole time the Lord Jesus was living among us, 22 beginning from John's baptism to the time when Jesus was taken up from
us. For one of these must become a witness with us of his resurrection."
23 So they nominated two men: Joseph called Barsabbas (also known as
Justus) and Matthias. 24 Then they prayed, "Lord, you know everyone's
heart. Show us which of these two you have chosen 25 to take over this
apostolic ministry, which Judas left to go where he belongs." 26 Then
they cast lots, and the lot fell to **Matthias**; so he **was added to the
eleven apostles.**

MT. PISGAH
BAPTIST CHURCH
TRUST YOURSELF
LESS
AND GOD
MORE
Sunday School
9:45
Worship Service
11:00 & 5:00
Pastor
Daniel Boutwell

18 WHAT IS THE GREAT COMMISSION?

Jesus' last instructions to His disciples prior to ascending into Heaven is considered the Great Commission

Matthew 28:18 Then Jesus came to them and said, "All authority in heav-
en and on earth has been given to me. 19 Therefore **go and make disciples of all nations**, baptizing them in the name of the Father and of the
Son and of the Holy Spirit, 20 and **teaching them to obey everything
I have commanded you.** And surely I am with you always, to the very
end of the age."

CHEAHA
BAPTIST CHURCH
JESUS SAID DON'T LET
YOUR HEART BE TROUBLED
BELIEVE IN GOD
SUNDAYSCHOOL
9:00AM
WORSHIP
10:00AM & 6:00PM
STEVEN JOHNSON
PASTOR

19 What Did Jesus Command?

Jesus Himself challenges us

John [14:15] "If you love me, keep my commands."

The last command called "The Great Commission" directs us to evangelize the world and teach what Jesus commanded.

Matthew [28:16] Then the eleven disciples went to Galilee, to the mountain where Jesus had told them to go. [17] When they saw him, they worshiped him; but some doubted. [18] Then Jesus came to them and said, "All authority in heaven and on earth has been given to me. [19] **Therefore go and make disciples of all nations, baptizing them in the name of the Father and of the Son and of the Holy Spirit,** [20] **and teaching them to obey everything I have commanded you.** And surely I am with you always, to the very end of the age."

If we are Christians, if we profess to follow Christ and His teachings, then we should learn what Jesus taught. What follows are the commands Jesus gave us:

The first recorded command of Jesus is for all to repent

Matthew [4:17] From that time on Jesus began to preach, **"Repent, for the kingdom of heaven has come near."**

And Jesus taught the need for individual repentance throughout his ministry

Luke [13:1] Now there were some present at that time who told Jesus about the Galileans whose blood Pilate had mixed with their sacrifices. [2] Jesus answered, "Do you think that these Galileans were worse sinners than all the other Galileans because they suffered this way? [3] I tell you, no! **But unless you repent, you too will all perish.**

Jesus was asked what are the two greatest commandments

Jesus' reply, found in Matthew:

Matthew 22:34 Hearing that Jesus had silenced the Sadducees, the Pharisees got together. 35 One of them, an expert in the law, tested him with this question:

36 "Teacher, which is the greatest commandment in the Law?"

Matthew 22:37 Jesus replied: **"'Love the Lord your God with all your heart and with all your soul and with all your mind.' 38 This is the first and greatest commandment. 39 And the second is like it: 'Love your neighbor as yourself.' 40 All the Law and the Prophets hang on these two commandments."**

His reply, found again in Mark:

Mark 12:28 One of the teachers of the law came and heard them debating. Noticing that Jesus had given them a good answer, he asked him, "Of all the commandments, which is the most important?" 29 **"The most important one," answered Jesus, "is this: 'Hear, O Israel, the Lord our God, the Lord is one. 30 Love the Lord your God with all your heart and with all your soul and with all your mind and with all your strength.' 31 The second is this: 'Love your neighbor as yourself.' There is no commandment greater than these."**

We are to learn from Jesus

Matthew 11:28 "Come to me, all you who are weary and burdened, and I will give you rest. 29 **Take my yoke upon you and learn from me,** for I am gentle and humble in heart, and you will find rest for your souls. 30 For my yoke is easy and my burden is light."

***Yoke**: a wooden crosspiece that is fastened over the necks of two animals and attached to the plow or cart that they are to pull*

We are to pray and never give up

Luke 18:1 Then Jesus told his disciples a parable to show them that they should always pray and not give up. 2 He said: "In a certain town there was a judge who neither feared God nor cared what people thought. 3 And there was a widow in that town who kept coming to him with the plea, 'Grant me justice against my adversary.' 4 For some time he refused. But finally he said to himself, 'Even though I don't fear God or care what people think, 5 yet because this widow keeps bothering me, I will see that she gets justice, so that she won't eventually come and attack me!'" 6 And the Lord said, "Listen to what the unjust judge says. 7 And **will not God bring about justice for his chosen ones, who cry out to him day and night?** Will he keep putting them off? 8 I tell you, he will see that they get justice, and quickly. However, **when the Son of Man comes, will he find faith on the earth?"**

The work of God is to keep faith

John 6:28 Then they asked him, "What must we do to do the works God requires?" Jesus answered, **"The work of God is this: to believe in the one he has sent."**

We are to trust in the light of the Lord

John 12:35 Then Jesus told them, "You are going to have the light just a little while longer. Walk while you have the light, before darkness overtakes you. Whoever walks in the dark does not know where they are going. **36 Believe in the light while you have the light, so that you may become children of light."** When he had finished speaking, Jesus left and hid himself from them.

We are instructed to remain in the love of Jesus

John 15:9 "As the Father has loved me, so have I loved you. **Now remain in my love. 10 If you keep my commands, you will remain in my love,** just as I have kept my Father's commands and remain in his love. 11 I have told you this so that my joy may be in you and that your joy may be complete."

We must do whatever is necessary to get sin out of our life

From Matthew:

Matthew 5:27 "You have heard that it was said, 'You shall not commit adultery.' 28 But I tell you that anyone who looks at a woman lustfully has already committed adultery with her in his heart. 29 **If your right eye causes you to stumble, gouge it out and throw it away.** It is better for you to lose one part of your body than for your whole body to be thrown into hell. 30 And **if your right hand causes you to stumble, cut it off and throw it away.** It is better for you to lose one part of your body than for your whole body to go into hell."

From Mark, with a warning:

Mark 9:42 "If anyone causes one of these little ones—those who believe in me—to stumble, it would be better for them if a large millstone were hung around their neck and they were thrown into the sea. 43 **If your hand causes you to stumble, cut it off. It is better for you to enter life maimed than with two hands to go into hell, where the fire never goes out.** 45 **And if your foot causes you to stumble, cut it off. It is better for you to enter life crippled than to have two feet and be thrown into hell.** 47 **And if your eye causes you to stumble, pluck it out.** It is better for you to enter the kingdom of God with one eye than to have two eyes and be thrown into hell, 48 where 'the worms that eat them do not die, and the fire is not quenched.' "

As followers of Christ we are to turn the other cheek

Matthew 5:38 "You have heard that it was said, 'Eye for eye, and tooth for tooth.' 39 But I tell you, **Do not resist an evil person. If anyone slaps you on the right cheek, turn to them the other cheek also.** 40 **And if anyone wants to sue you and take your shirt, hand over your coat as well.** 41 **If anyone forces you to go one mile, go with them two miles.** 42 **Give to the one who asks you, and do not turn away from the one who wants to borrow from you."**

Luke 6:27 "But **to you who are listening I say: Love your enemies, do good to those who hate you,** 28 **bless those who curse you, pray for**

those who mistreat you. 29 If someone slaps you on one cheek, turn to them the other also. If someone takes your coat, do not withhold your shirt from them. 30 Give to everyone who asks you, and if anyone takes what belongs to you, do not demand it back."

We are not to fear man

Luke 12:4 "I tell you, my friends, **do not be afraid of those who kill the body** and after that can do no more."

We are to fear one

Luke 12:5 "But I will show you whom you should fear: **Fear him who, after your body has been killed, has authority to throw you into hell.** Yes, I tell you, fear him."

In our fear we are to know God will protect us

Luke 12:6 "Are not five sparrows sold for two pennies? Yet not one of them is forgotten by God. 7 **Indeed, the very hairs of your head are all numbered. Don't be afraid; you are worth more than many sparrows."**

Have faith in God and do not let you heart be troubled

Mark 11:22 **"Have faith in God,"** Jesus answered. 23 "Truly I tell you, if anyone says to this mountain, 'Go, throw yourself into the sea,' and does not doubt in their heart but believes that what they say will happen, it will be done for them. 24 Therefore I tell you, whatever you ask for in prayer, believe that you have received it, and it will be yours. 25 And when you stand praying, if you hold anything against anyone, forgive him, so that your Father in heaven may forgive you your sins."

John 14:1 **"Do not let your hearts be troubled. You believe in God; believe also in me.** 2 In my Father's house are many rooms; if it were not so, I would have told you. I am going there to prepare a place for you. 3 And if I go and prepare a place for you, I will come back and take you to be with me that you also may be where I am."

John 14:25 "All this I have spoken while still with you. 26 But the Advocate, the Holy Spirit, whom the Father will send in my name, will teach you all things and will remind you of everything I have said to you. 27 **Peace I leave with you; my peace I give you. I do not give to you as the world gives. Do not let your hearts be troubled and do not be afraid."**

We are to be merciful

Luke 6:32 "If you love those who love you, what credit is that to you? Even 'sinners' love those who love them. 33 And if you do good to those who are good to you, what credit is that to you? Even 'sinners' do that. 34 And if you lend to those from whom you expect repayment, what credit is that to you? Even 'sinners' lend to 'sinners,' expecting to be repaid in full. 35 But love your enemies, do good to them, and lend to them without expecting to get anything back. Then your reward will be great, and you will be children of the Most High, because he is kind to the ungrateful and wicked. 36 **Be merciful, just as your Father is merciful."**

We are not to judge others

Matthew 7:1 **"Do not judge**, or you too will be judged. 2 For in the same way you judge others, you will be judged, and with the measure you use, it will be measured to you."

We are not to worry

Matthew 6:25 "Therefore I tell you, **do not worry about your life**, what you will eat or drink; or about your body, what you will wear. Is not life more important than food, and the body more important than clothes? 26 Look at the birds of the air; they do not sow or reap or store away in barns, and yet your heavenly Father feeds them. Are you not much more valuable than they? 27 Can any one of you by worrying add a single hour to his life? 28 And why do you worry about clothes? See how the flowers of the field grow. They do not labor or spin. 29 Yet I tell you that not even Solomon in all his splendor was dressed like one of these. 30 If that is how God clothes the grass of the field, which is here today and tomorrow is thrown into the fire, will he not much more clothe you—

you of little faith? 31 **So do not worry,** saying, 'What shall we eat?' or 'What shall we drink?' or 'What shall we wear?' 32 For the pagans run after all these things, and your heavenly Father knows that you need them. 33 But **seek first his kingdom and his righteousness,** and all these things will be given to you as well. 34 Therefore do not worry about tomorrow, for tomorrow will worry about itself. Each day has enough trouble of its own."

Luke 12:22 Then Jesus said to his disciples: "Therefore I tell you, **do not worry about your life, what you will eat; or about your body, what you will wear.** 23 Life is more than food, and the body more than clothes. 24 Consider the ravens: They do not sow or reap, they have no storeroom or barn; yet God feeds them. And how much more valuable you are than birds! 25 Who of you by worrying can add a single hour to his life? 26 Since you cannot do this very little thing, why do you worry about the rest?"

Luke 12:27 "Consider how the wild flowers grow. They do not labor or spin. Yet I tell you, not even Solomon in all his splendor was dressed like one of these. 28 If that is how God clothes the grass of the field, which is here today, and tomorrow is thrown into the fire, how much more will he clothe you—you of little faith! 29 And **do not set your heart on what you will eat or drink; do not worry about it.** 30 For the pagan world runs after all such things, and your Father knows that you need them. 31 **But seek his kingdom, and these things will be given to you as well."**

Do not be greedy

Luke 12:13 Someone in the crowd said to him, "Teacher, tell my brother to divide the inheritance with me." 14 Jesus replied, "Man, who appointed me a judge or an arbiter between you?" 15 Then he said to them, **"Watch out! Be on your guard against all kinds of greed; life does not consist in an abundance of possessions."**

Sell your possessions and give to the poor

Luke 12:32 "Do not be afraid, little flock, for your Father has been pleased to give you the kingdom. 33 **Sell your possessions and give to the poor.**

Provide purses for yourselves that will not wear out, a treasure in heaven that will not be exhausted, where no thief comes near and no moth destroys. [34] For **where your treasure is, there your heart will be also."**

We are to feed the poor

Luke [14:12] Then Jesus said to his host, "When you give a luncheon or dinner, do not invite your friends, your brothers or sisters, your relatives, or your rich neighbors; if you do, they may invite you back and so you will be repaid. [13] But **when you give a banquet, invite the poor, the crippled, the lame, the blind,** [14] **and you will be blessed.** Although they cannot repay you, you will be repaid at the resurrection of the righteous."

Do not seek recognition for your giving

Matthew [6:2] "So when you give to the needy, do not announce it with trumpets, as the hypocrites do in the synagogues and on the streets, to be honored by others. Truly I tell you, they have received their reward in full. [3] **But when you give to the needy, do not let your left hand know what your right hand is doing,** [4] **so that your giving may be in secret.** Then your Father, who sees what is done in secret, will reward you."

We are to store heavenly treasures

Matthew [6:19] **"Do not store up for yourselves treasures on earth, where moths and vermin destroy, and where thieves break in and steal.** [20] **But store up for yourselves treasures in heaven,** where moths and vermin do not destroy, and where thieves do not break in and steal. [21] For where your treasure is, there your heart will be also."

Jesus taught we are to pay taxes and tithe

Matthew [22:15] Then the Pharisees went out and laid plans to trap him in his words. [16] They sent their disciples to him along with the Herodians. "Teacher," they said, "we know you are a man of integrity and that you teach the way of God in accordance with the truth. You aren't swayed by others, because you pay no attention to who they are. [17] Tell us then, what is your opinion? Is it right to pay the imperial tax to Caesar or not?"[18] But Jesus, knowing their evil intent, said, "You hypocrites, why are you trying to trap me? [19] Show me the coin used for paying the tax." They brought him a denarius, [20] and he asked them, "Whose image is this? And whose inscription?" [21] "Caesar's," they replied. Then he said to them, "**Give to Caesar what is Caesar's, and to God what is God's.**"

Treat others the way you want to be treated

Luke [6:27] "But to you who are listening I say: Love your enemies, do good to those who hate you, [28] bless those who curse you, pray for those who mistreat you. [29] If someone slaps you on one cheek, turn to them the other also. If someone takes your coat, do not withhold your shirt from them. [30] Give to everyone who asks you, and if anyone takes what belongs to you, do not demand it back. [31] **Do to others as you would have them do to you.**"

We are to make peace

Matthew [5:23] "Therefore, if you are offering your gift at the altar and there remember that your brother or sister has something against you, [24] leave your gift there in front of the altar. First **go and be reconciled to them; then come and offer your gift.**"

Mark [9:50] "Salt is good, but if it loses its saltiness, how can you make it salty again? **Have salt amoung yourselves, and be at peace with each other.**"

We are to love our enemies

Matthew [5:43] "You have heard that it was said, 'Love your neighbor and hate your enemy.' [44] But I tell you**: Love your enemies and pray for those who persecute you**, [45] that you may be children of your Father in heaven. He causes his sun to rise on the evil and the good, and sends rain on the righteous and the unrighteous. [46] If you love those who love you, what reward will you get? Are not even the tax collectors doing that? [47] And if you greet only your own people, what are you doing more than others? Do not even pagans do that?"

Luke [6:27] "But to you who are listening I say: **Love your enemies, do good to those who hate you,** [28] bless those who curse you, pray for those who mistreat you. [29] If someone slaps you on one cheek, turn to them the other also. If someone takes your coat, do not withhold your shirt from him. [30] Give to everyone who asks you, and if anyone takes what belongs to you, do not demand it back. [31] **Do to others as you would have them do to you."**

Luke [6:32] "If you love those who love you, what credit is that to you? Even sinners love those who love them. [33] And if you do good to those who are good to you, what credit is that to you? Even sinners do that. [34] And if you lend to those from whom you expect repayment, what credit is that to you? Even sinners lend to sinners, expecting to be repaid in full. [35] **But love your enemies, do good to them, and lend to them without expecting to get anything back.** Then your reward will be great, and you will be children of the Most High, because he is kind to the ungrateful and wicked. [36] **Be merciful, just as your Father is merciful."**

We should seek perfection in our love

Matthew [5:48] **Be perfect, therefore, as your heavenly Father is perfect.**

We are to forgive our fellow man

Matthew [18:21] Then Peter came to Jesus and asked, "Lord, **how many times shall I forgive my brother or sister when he sins against me? Up to seven times?"** [22] **Jesus answered, "I tell you, not seven times, but seventy-seven times."**

Mark [11:25] And when you stand praying, **if you hold anything against anyone, forgive them,** so that your Father in heaven may forgive you your sins.

Luke [17:3] So watch yourselves. **If your brother or sister sins against you, rebuke them, and if they repent, forgive them.** [4] **Even if they sin against you seven times in a day, and seven times comes back to you saying, "I repent," you must forgive them.**

We are to seek the narrow gate

Matthew [7:13] **Enter through the narrow gate**. For wide is the gate and broad is the road that leads to destruction, and many enter through it. [14] But small is the gate and narrow the road that leads to life, and only a few find it.

Luke [13:22] Then Jesus went through the towns and villages, teaching as he made his way to Jerusalem. [23] Someone asked him, "Lord, are only a few people going to be saved?" He said to them, [24] "**Make every effort to enter through the narrow door,** because many, I tell you, will try to enter and will not be able to."

Watch out for false prophets

Matthew [7:15] **Watch out for false prophets**. They come to you in sheep's clothing, but inwardly they are ferocious wolves. [16] By their fruit you will recognize them.

Matthew [24:4] Jesus answered: **"Watch out that no one deceives you.** [5] For many will come in my name, claiming, 'I am the Messiah,' and will deceive many."

Luke [21:8] He replied: "**Watch out that you are not deceived**. For many will come in my name, claiming, 'I am he,' and, 'The time is near.' **Do not follow them**. [9] When you hear of wars and uprisings, do not be frightened. These things must happen first, but the end will not come right away."

We are not to swear

Matthew [5:33] Again, you have heard that it was said to the people long ago, "Do not break your oath, but fulfill to the Lord the vows you have made." [34] But I tell you, **Do not swear at all: either by heaven, for it is God's throne; [35] or by the earth, for it is his footstool; or by Jerusalem, for it is the city of the Great King. [36] And do not swear by your head, for you cannot make even one hair white or black. [37] All you need to say is simply "Yes" or"No"; anything beyond this comes from the evil one.**

No one is to be called 'Father' and no one is to be called 'Instructor'

Matthew [23:8] But you are not to be called "Rabbi," for you have only one Teacher and you are all brothers. [9] **And do not call anyone on earth "father," for you have one Father, and he is in heaven.** [10] **Nor are you to be called ""instructor," for you have one instructor, the Messiah.**

Do not divorce

Mark [10:5] "It was because your hearts were hard that Moses wrote you this law," Jesus replied. [6] "But at the beginning of creation God 'made them male and female. [7] **For this reason a man will leave his father and mother and be united to his wife,** [8] **and the two will become one flesh.' So they are no longer two, but one flesh.** [9] **Therefore what God has joined together, let no one separate."**

We are to love each other

John [13:34] **A new command I give you: Love one another. As I have loved you, so you must love one another.** [35] **By this everyone will know that you are my disciples, if you love one another.**

John [15:12] **My command is this: Love each other as I have loved you.** [13] Greater love has no one than this, to lay down one's life for one's friends. [14] You are my friends if you do what I command. [15] I no longer call you servants, because a servant does not know his master's business. Instead, I have called you friends, for everything that I learned from my Father I have made known to you. [16] You did not choose me, but I chose you and appointed you so you might go and bear fruit—fruit that will last—and so that whatever you ask in my name the Father will give you. [17] **This is my command: Love each other.**

Go into the world and preach

Mark [16:15] He said to them, **"Go into all the world and preach the gospel to all creation.** [16] Whoever believes and is baptized will be saved, but whoever does not believe will be condemned. [17] And these signs will accompany those who believe: In my name they will drive out demons; they will speak in new tongues; [18] they will pick up snakes with their hands; and when they drink deadly poison, it will not hurt them at all; they will place their hands on sick people, and they will get well."

Be obedient and humble servants to the Lord

Luke [17:7] Suppose one of you had a servant plowing or looking after the sheep. Would he say to the servant when he comes in from the field, "Come along now and sit down to eat"? [8] Would he not rather say, "Prepare my supper, get yourself ready and wait on me while I eat and drink; after that you may eat and drink"? [9] Will he thank the servant because he did what he was told to do? [10] **So you also, when you have done everything you were told to do, should say, "We are unworthy servants; we have only done our duty."**

John [13:12] When he had finished washing their feet, he put on his clothes and returned to his place. "Do you understand what I have done for you?" he asked them. [13] "You call me 'Teacher' and 'Lord,' and rightly so, for that is what I am. [14] **Now that I, your Lord and Teacher, have washed your feet, you also should wash one another's feet.** [15] **I have set you an example that you should do as I have done for you.** [16] Very truly I tell you, no servant is greater than his master, nor is a messenger greater than the one who sent him. [17] Now that you know these things, you will be blessed if you do them."

At all times be ready for Christ's return

Luke [12:35] Be dressed ready for service and keep your lamps burning, [36] like servants waiting for their master to return from a wedding banquet, so that when he comes and knocks they can immediately open the door for him. [37] It will be good for those servants whose master finds them watching when he comes. Truly I tell you, he will dress himself to serve, will have them recline at the table and will come and wait on them. [38] It will be good for those servants whose master finds them ready, even if he comes in the middle of the night or toward daybreak. [39] But understand this: If the owner of the house had known at what hour the thief was coming, he would not have let his house be broken into. [40] **You also must be ready, because the Son of Man will come at an hour when you do not expect him.**

Mark [13:35] Therefore keep watch because you do not know when the
owner of the house will come back—whether in the evening, or at midnight, or when the rooster crows, or at dawn. [36] If he comes suddenly,
do not let him find you sleeping. [37] **What I say to you, I say to everyone: "Watch!"**

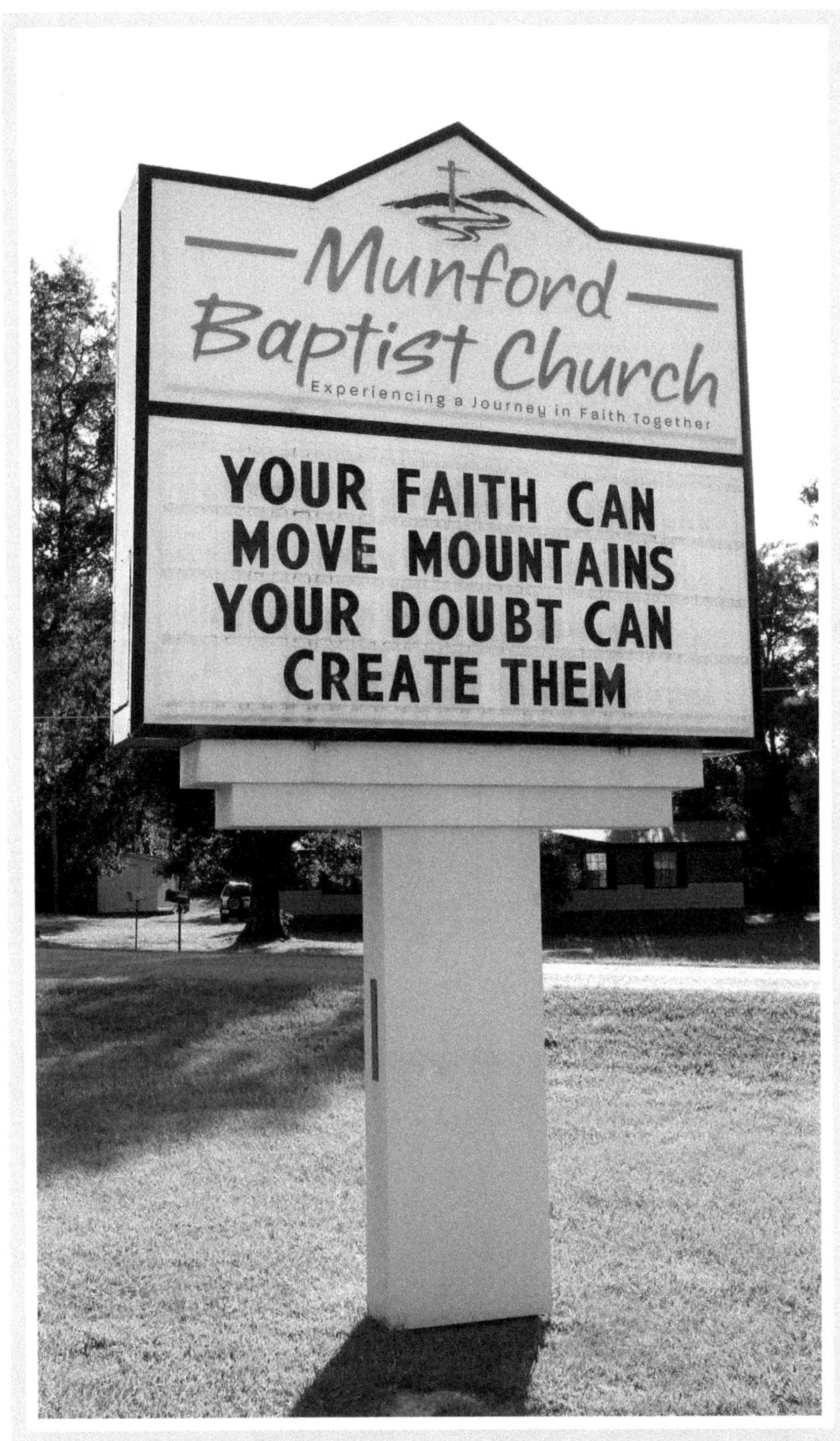
Munford
Baptist Church
Experiencing a Journey in Faith Together
YOUR FAITH CAN
MOVE MOUNTAINS
YOUR DOUBT CAN
CREATE THEM

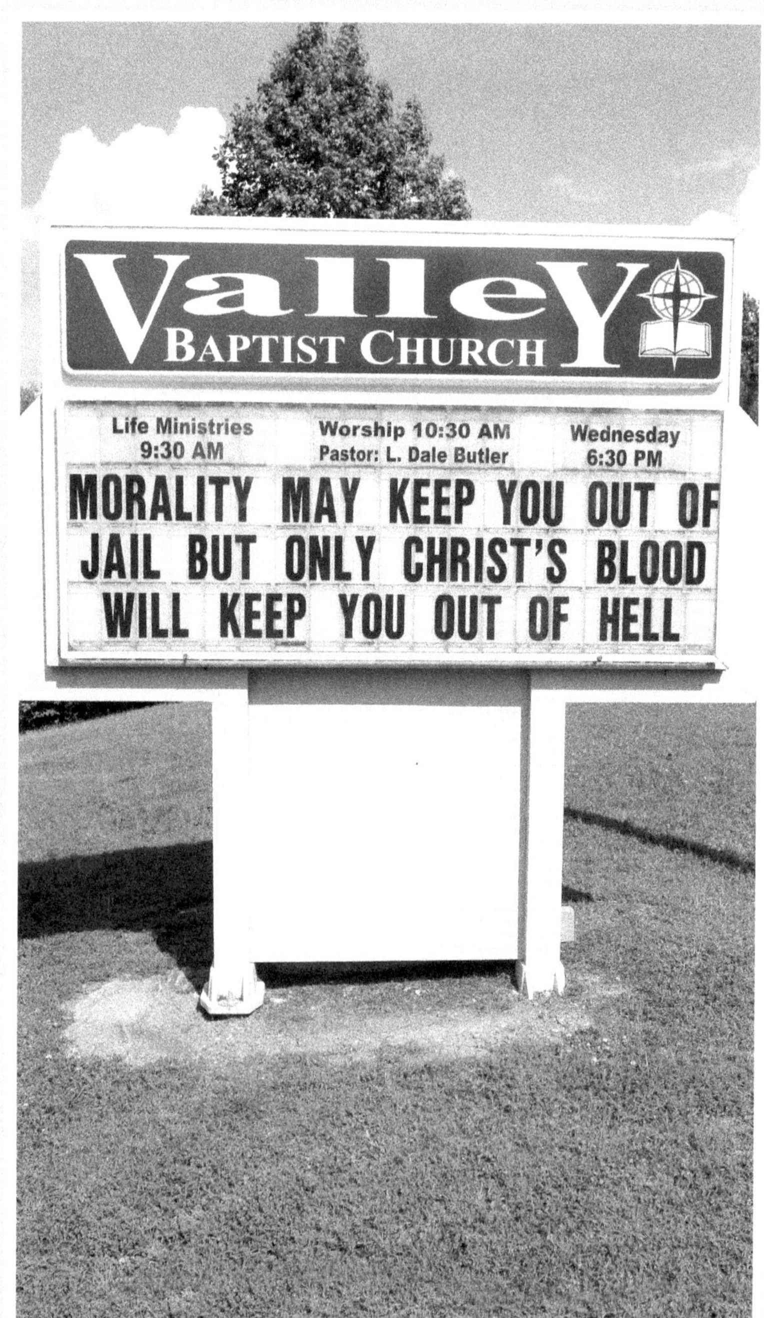
Valley
BAPTIST CHURCH
Life Ministries
9:30 AM
Worship 10:30 AM
Pastor: L. Dale Butler
Wednesday
6:30 PM
MORALITY MAY KEEP YOU OUT OF
JAIL BUT ONLY CHRIST'S BLOOD
WILL KEEP YOU OUT OF HELL

20 What is Jesus Doing now?

Jesus is with us

Matthew 28:16 Then the eleven disciples went to Galilee, to the mountain where Jesus had told them to go. 17 When they saw him, they worshiped him; but some doubted. 18 Then Jesus came to them and said, **"All authority in heaven and on earth has been given to me.** 19 Therefore go and make disciples of all nations, baptizing them in the name of the Father and of the Son and of the Holy Spirit, 20 and teaching them to obey everything I have commanded you. And surely **I am with you always, to the very end of the age."**

Jesus also is in Heaven with God

Luke 24:50 When he had led them out to the vicinity of Bethany, he lifted up his hands and blessed them. 51 **While he was blessing them, he left them and was taken up into heaven.** 52 Then they worshiped him and returned to Jerusalem with great joy. 53 And they stayed continually at the temple, praising God.

Mark 16:19 After the Lord Jesus had spoken to them, **he was taken up into heaven and he sat at the right hand of God.** 20 Then the disciples went out and preached everywhere, and the Lord worked with them and confirmed his word by the signs that accompanied it.

Jesus is preparing a place for believers

John 14:1 Do not let your hearts be troubled. You believe in God; **believe** also in me. 2 My Father's house has many rooms; if that were not so, would I have told you **that I am going there to prepare a place for you?** 3 And if I go and prepare a place for you, **I will come back and take you to be with me** that you also may be where I am.

BETHEL MISSIONARY
BAPTIST CHURCH
LIVE LIKE
HE'S COMING
BACK TODAY
SUNDAY SCHOOL 9:30 MORNING WORSHIP 10:45
WEDNESDAY MEETING 6:00
REV. ANGELO GROCE, PASTOR

21

Who Knows When Jesus Will Return?

Only God Himself knows

Matthew 24:36 But about that day or hour no one knows, not even the angels in heaven, nor the Son, but only the Father. 37 As it was in the days of Noah, so it will be at the coming of the Son of Man. 38 For in the days before the flood, people were eating and drinking, marrying and giving in marriage, up to the day Noah entered the ark; 39 and they knew nothing about what would happen until the flood came and took them all away. That is how it will be at the coming of the Son of Man. 40 Two men will be in the field; one will be taken and the other left. 41 Two women will be grinding with a hand mill; one will be taken and the other left. 42 Therefore keep watch, because you do not know on what day your Lord will come. 43 But understand this: If the owner of the house had known at what time of night the thief was coming, he would have kept watch and would not have let his house be broken into. 44 So you also must be ready, because **the Son of Man will come at an hour when you do not expect him.**

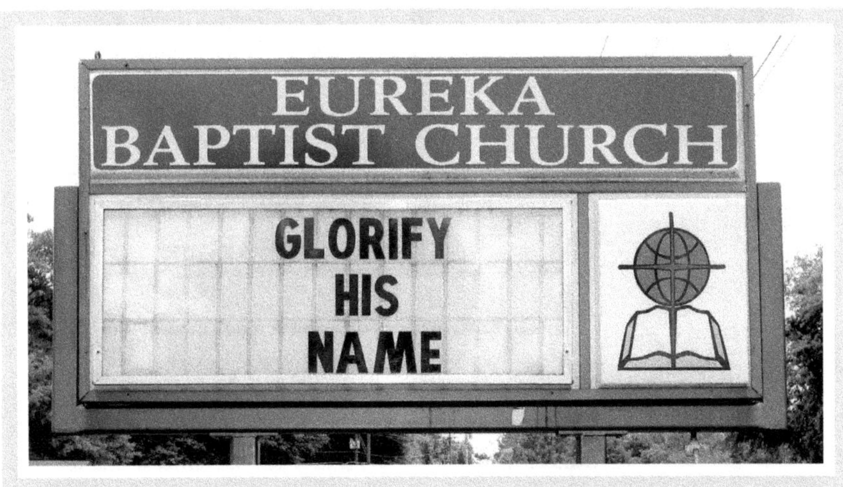

MIRACLE REVIVAL
TEMPLE
CHRIST'S RETURN
IS NEAR - DON'T
MISS IT FOR
THE WORLD!

22

What does the Bible say about the time of Jesus' Return?

Jesus said watch for these signs

Mark 13:1 As Jesus was leaving the temple, one of his disciples said to him, "Look, Teacher! What massive stones! What magnificent buildings!" 2 "Do you see all these great buildings?" replied Jesus. "Not one stone here will be left on another; every one will be thrown down." 3 As Jesus was sitting on the Mount of Olives opposite the temple, Peter, James, John and Andrew asked him privately, 4 **"Tell us, when will these things happen? And what will be the sign that they are all about to be fulfilled?"**

Mark 13:5 Jesus said to them: **"Watch out that no one deceives you.** 6 Many will come in my name, claiming, 'I am he,' and will deceive many. 7 When you hear of wars and rumors of wars, do not be alarmed. Such things must happen, but the end is still to come. 8 Nation will rise against nation, and kingdom against kingdom. There will be earthquakes in various places, and famines. These are the beginning of birth pains.

Mark 13:9 You must be on your guard. You will be handed over to the local councils and flogged in the synagogues. On account of me you will stand before governors and kings as witnesses to them. 10 **And the gospel must first be preached to all nations.** 11 Whenever you are arrested and brought to trial, do not worry beforehand about what to say. Just say whatever is given you at the time, for it is not you speaking, but the Holy Spirit.

Mark 13:12 **Brother will betray brother to death, and a father his child. Children will rebel against their parents and have them put to death.** 13 **Everyone will hate you because of me,** but he who stands firm to the end will be saved.

Mark 13:14 **When you see "the abomination that causes desolation"**
standing where it does not belong— let the reader understand—then
let those who are in Judea flee to the mountains. 15 Let no one on the
roof of his house go down or enter the house to take anything out. 16 Let
no one in the field go back to get his cloak. 17 How dreadful it will be in
those days for pregnant women and nursing mothers! 18 Pray that this
will not take place in winter, 19 because **those will be days of distress**
unequaled from the beginning, when God created the world, until
now—and never to be equaled again. 20 If the Lord had not cut short
those days, no one would survive. But for the sake of the elect, whom
he has chosen, he has shortened them. 21 At that time if anyone says to
you, "Look, here is the Messiah!" or, "Look, there he is!" do not believe
it. 22 **For false messiahs and false prophets will appear and perform**
signs and miracles to deceive, if possible, even the elect. 23 So be on
your guard; I have told you everything ahead of time.

Mark 13:24 But in those days, following that distress, "the sun will be
darkened, and the moon will not give its light; 25 the stars will fall from
the sky, and the heavenly bodies will be shaken." 26 **At that time peo-**
ple will see the Son of Man coming in clouds with great power and
glory. 27 And he will send his angels and gather his elect from the four
winds, from the ends of the earth to the ends of the heavens.

Mark 13:28 Now learn this lesson from the fig tree: As soon as its twigs
get tender and its leaves come out, you know that summer is near. 29
Even so, when you see these things happening, you know that it is near,
right at the door. 30 **Truly I tell you, this generation will certainly not**
pass away until all these things have happened. 31 **Heaven and earth**
will pass away, but my words will never pass away.

Peter wrote about the time of Jesus' return

2 Peter 3:3 Above all, you must understand that **in the last days** scoffers
will come, scoffing and following their own evil desires. 4 They will say,
"Where is this 'coming' he promised? Ever since our ancestors died,
everything goes on as it has since the beginning of creation." 5 But they
deliberately forget that long ago by God's word the heavens existed and
the earth was formed out of water and by water. 6 By these waters also

the world of that time was deluged and destroyed. [7] By the same word **the present heavens and earth are reserved for fire, being kept for the day of judgment and destruction of the ungodly.**

2 Peter [3:8] But do not forget this one thing, dear friends: **With the Lord a day is like a thousand years, and a thousand years are like a day.** [9] The Lord is not slow in keeping his promise, as some understand slowness. He is patient with you, not wanting anyone to perish, but everyone to come to repentance.

2 Peter [3:10] But **the day of the Lord will come like a thief. The heavens will disappear with a roar; the elements will be destroyed by fire, and the earth and everything done in it will be laid bare.**

And Paul wrote to Timothy about Jesus' return

2 Timothy [3:1] But mark this: **There will be terrible times in the last days.** [2] People will be lovers of themselves, lovers of money, boastful, proud, abusive, disobedient to their parents, ungrateful, unholy, [3] without love, unforgiving, slanderous, without self-control, brutal, not lovers of the good, [4] treacherous, rash, conceited, lovers of pleasure rather than lovers of God— [5] having a form of godliness but denying its power. Have nothing to do with such people. [6] They are the kind who worm their way into homes and gain control over gullible women, who are loaded down with sins and are swayed by all kinds of evil desires, [7] always learning but never able to come to a knowledge of the truth.

HARMONY
BAPTIST CHURCH
LET GOD'S LOVE
SHINE
THROUGH YOU
Sunday School 8:45 • Morning Worship 10:00 • Evening Worship 6:00
Wednesday 6:00 PASTOR: Rev. David Jones

23 What are we to do until Jesus returns?

Watch, be patient, and stand firm

Mark [13:32] **But about that day or hour, no one knows, not even the angels in heaven, nor the Son, but only the Father.** [33] **Be on guard! Be alert! You do not know when that time will come.** [34] It's like a man going away: He leaves his house and puts his servants in charge, each with his assigned task, and tells the one at the door to keep watch.

Mark [13:35] Therefore keep watch because you do not know when the owner of the house will come back— whether in the evening, or at midnight, or when the rooster crows, or at dawn. [36] If he comes suddenly, do not let him find you sleeping. [37] **What I say to you, I say to everyone: "Watch!"**

James [5:7] Be patient, then, brothers and sisters, until the Lord's coming. See how the farmer waits for the land to yield its valuable crop patiently waiting for the autumn and spring rains. [8] You too, **be patient and stand firm, because the Lord's coming is near.** [9] Don't grumble against one another, brothers and sisters, or you will be judged. The Judge is standing at the door!

Zion
BAPTIST CHURCH
STOP WORRYING
GOD'S GOT IT

24 What should I worry about?

Jesus told us of the foolishness of worry

Matthew 6:25 Therefore I tell you, **do not worry about your life, what you will eat or drink; or about your body, what you will wear.** Is not life more important than food, and the body more important than clothes? 26 Look at the birds of the air; they do not sow or reap or store away in barns, and yet your heavenly Father feeds them. Are you not much more valuable than they? 27 **Can any one of you by worrying add a single hour to his life?** 6:28 And why do you worry about clothes? See how the flowers of the field grow. They do not labor or spin. 29 Yet I tell you that not even Solomon in all his splendor was dressed like one of these. 30 If that is how God clothes the grass of the field, which is here today and tomorrow is thrown into the fire, will he not much more clothe you—**you of little faith?** 31 **So do not worry, saying, "What shall we eat?" or '"What shall we drink?" or "What shall we wear?"** 32 For the pagans run after all these things, and your heavenly Father knows that you need them. 33 **But seek first his kingdom and his righteousness, and all these things will be given to you as well.** 34 **Therefore do not worry about tomorrow, for tomorrow will worry about itself.** Each day has enough trouble of its own.

McCauley's Chapel
UNITED METHODIST CHURCH
FORBIDDEN FRUITS
CREATE
MANY JAMS
-PASTOR-
REV. CURTIS SCOTT
SUNDAY SCHOOL 10:00AM
MORNING WORSHIP 11:00AM
EVENING WORSHIP 5:30PM
824
Tabor Road

25 What type of treasure should I seek?

Jesus told us to look to heaven

Matthew 6:19 Do not store up for yourselves treasures on earth, where moths and vermin destroy, and where thieves break in and steal. 20 **But store up for yourselves treasures in heaven,** where moths and vermin do not destroy, and where thieves do not break in and steal. 21 For **where your treasure is, there your heart will be also.**

COOSA VALLEY
BAPTIST CHURCH
THE HOLY SPIRIT - GOD'S
PROMISE TO THE CHURCH
SUNDAY SCHOOL
9:45 A.M.
WORSHIP SERVICE
11:00 A.M.

26 What Do We Know About the Holy Spirit?

A psalmist wrote about the Holy Spirit

Psalm 51:10 Create in me a pure heart, O God, and renew a steadfast spirit within me. 11 **Do not cast me from your presence or take your Holy Spirit from me.** 12 Restore to me the joy of your salvation and grant me a willing spirit, to sustain me.

The Holy Spirit conceived Christ in Mary

Matthew 1:18 This is how the birth of Jesus the Messiah came about: His mother Mary was pledged to be married to Joseph, but before they came together, **she was found to be pregnant through the Holy Spirit.** 19 Because Joseph her husband was faithful to the law, and yet he did not want to expose her to public disgrace, he had in mind to divorce her quietly. 20 But after he had considered this, an angel of the Lord appeared to him in a dream and said, "Joseph son of David, do not be afraid to take Mary home as your wife, because **what is conceived in her is from the Holy Spirit.** 21 She will give birth to a son, and you are to give him the name Jesus, because he will save his people from their sins."

The Holy Spirit is sent by God and lives within Christians

John 14:15 If you love me, keep my commands. 16 And I will ask the Father, and **he will give you another advocate to help you and be with you forever—** 17 **the Spirit of truth.** The world cannot accept him, because it neither sees him nor knows him. But you know him, for **he lives with you and will be in you.**

1 Corinthians 3:16 Don't you know that **you yourselves are God's temple and that God's Spirit dwells in your midst?** 17 If anyone destroys God's temple, God will destroy that person; for God's temple is sacred, and you together are that temple.

The Holy Spirit comes to Christians

Acts 2:38 Peter replied, **"Repent and be baptized, every one of you, in the name of Jesus Christ for the forgiveness of your sins. And you will receive the gift of the Holy Spirit.** 39 The promise is for you and your children and for all who are far off—for all whom the Lord our God will call."

1 Corinthians 12:12 Just as a body, though one, has many parts; but all its many parts form one body. So it is with Christ. 13 For **we were all baptized by one Spirit so as to form one body**—whether Jews or Gentiles, slave or free—and we were all given the one Spirit to drink.

The Spirit is a Counselor and Teacher

John 14:25 All this I have spoken while still with you. 26 **But the Advocate, the Holy Spirit, whom the Father will send in my name, will teach you all things and will remind you of everything I have said to you.**

John 16:12 I have much more to say to you, more than you can now bear. 13 **But when he, the Spirit of truth, comes, he will guide you into all truth**. He will not speak on his own; he will speak only what he hears, and he will tell you what is yet to come. 14 He will glorify me because it is from me that he will receive what he will make known unto you. 15 All that belongs to the Father is mine. That is why I said the Spirit will receive from me what he will make it known to you.

1 Corinthians 2: 9 However, as it is written: "What no eye has seen, what no ear has heard, and what no human mind has conceived"—the things God has prepared for those who love him—these are the things God has revealed to us by the Spirit.

1 Corinthians 2:10 these are the things **God has revealed it to us by his Spirit. The Spirit searches all things, even the deep things of God.** 11 For who knows a person's thoughts except their own spirit within them? In the same way no one knows the thoughts of God except the Spirit of God. 12 **What we have received is not the spirit of the world, but the Spirit who is from God, so that we may understand what God**

has freely given us. [13] This is what we speak, not in words taught us by human wisdom but **in words taught by the Spirit, explaining spiritual realities with Spirit-taught words.** [14] The person without the Spirit does not accept the things that come from the Spirit of God but considers them foolishness, and cannot understand them because they are discerned only through the Spirit. [15] The person with the Spirit makes judgments about all things, but such a person is not subject to merely human judgments.

The Holy Spirit confirms Christ is Lord

John [15:26] When the Advocate comes, whom I will send to you from the Father—the Spirit of truth who goes out from the Father— **he will testify about me.**

1 Corinthians [12:1] Now about spiritual gifts, brothers and sisters, I do not want you to be uninformed. [2] You know that when you were pagans, somehow or other you were influenced and led astray to mute idols. [3] Therefore I want you to know that no one who is speaking by the Spirit of God says, "Jesus be cursed," and **no one can say, "Jesus is Lord," except by the Holy Spirit.**

The Holy Spirit provides spiritual gifts

1 Corinthians [12:4] There are different kinds of gifts, but the same Spirit distributes them. [5] There are different kinds of service, but the same Lord. [6] There are different kinds of working, but in all of them and in everyone it is the same God at work.

1 Corinthians [12:7] Now to each one the manifestation of the Spirit is given for the common good. [8] To one there is given through the Spirit the message of **wisdom**, to another the message of **knowledge** by means of the same Spirit, [9] to another **faith** by the same Spirit, to another gifts of **healing** by that one Spirit, [10] to another **miraculous powers**, to another **prophecy**, to another **distinguishing between spirits**, to another speaking in different kinds of **tongues**, and to still another the **interpretation of tongues.** [11] All these are the work of one and the same Spirit, and **he distributes them to each one, just as he determines.**

The Holy Spirit inspires specific character traits in Christians

Galatians 5:22 But the fruit of the Spirit is **love, joy, peace, forbearance, kindness, goodness, faithfulness,** 23 **gentleness and self-control.** Against such things there is no law. 24 Those who belong to Christ Jesus have crucified the flesh with its passions and desires. 25 **Since we live by the Spirit, let us keep in step with the Spirit.** 26 Let us not become conceited, provoking and envying each other.

Ephesians 5:15 Be very careful, then, how you live—not as unwise but as wise, 16 making the most of every opportunity, because the days are evil. 17 Therefore do not be foolish, but **understand what the Lord's will is.** 18 Do not get drunk on wine, which leads to debauchery. Instead, **be filled with the Spirit.** 19 **Speak to one another with psalms, hymns and songs from the Spirit. Sing and make music from your heart to the Lord,** 20 **always giving thanks to God the Father for everything, in the name of our Lord Jesus Christ.**

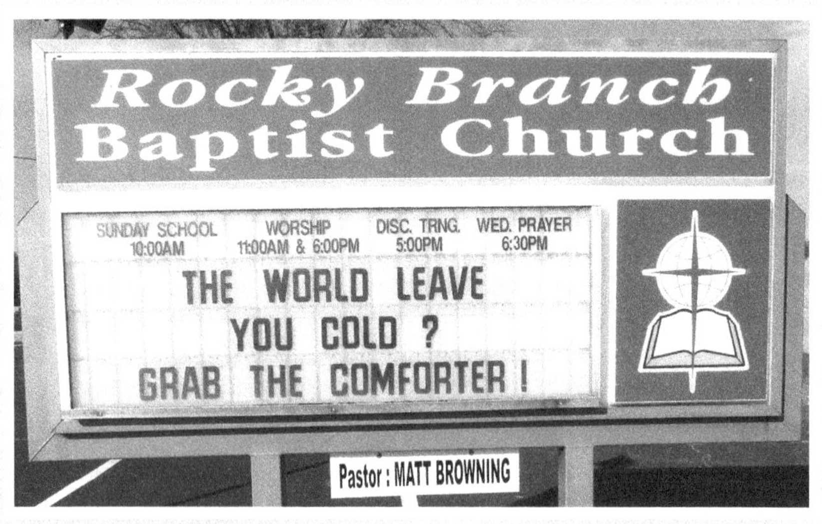

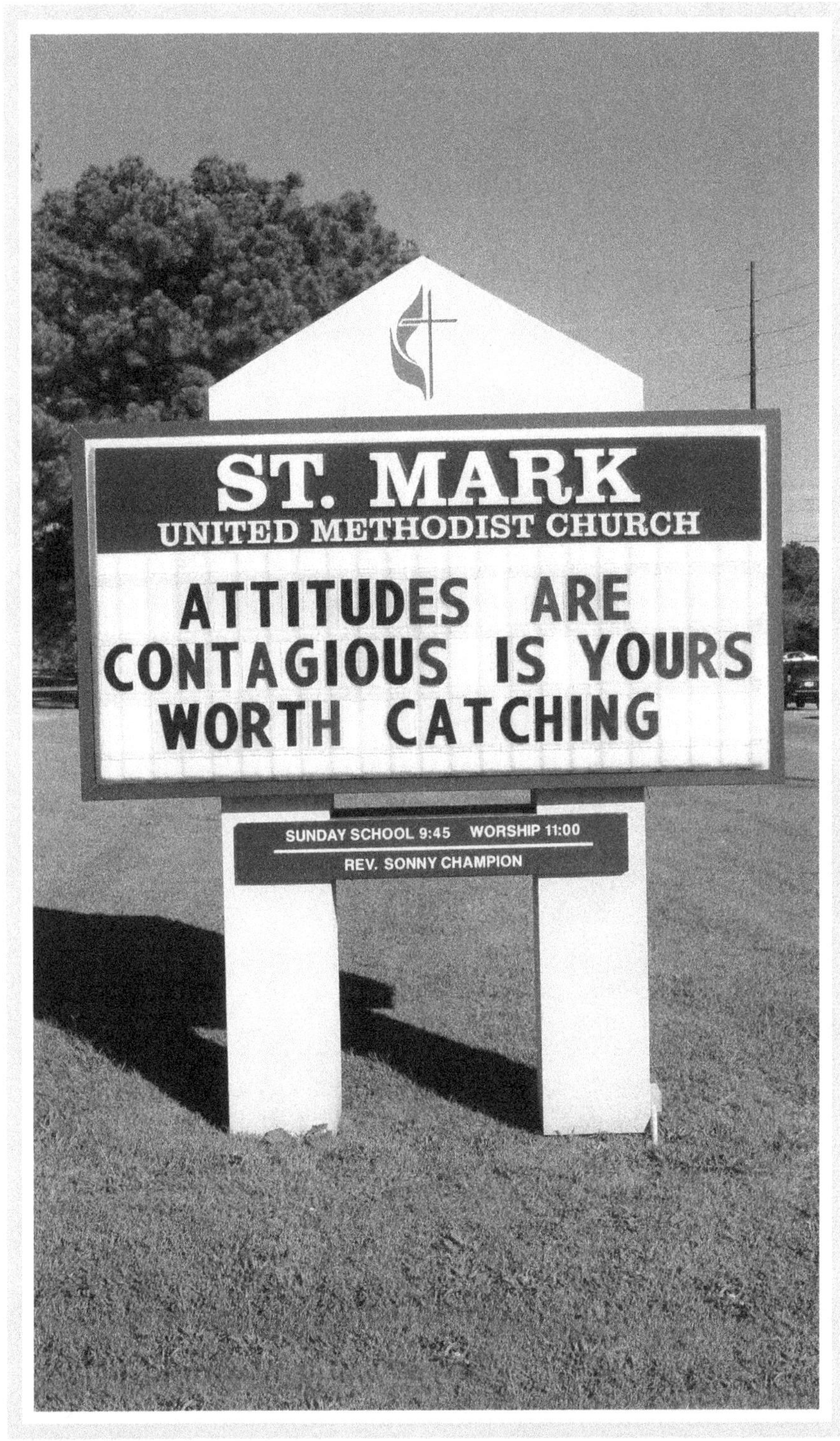
ST. MARK
UNITED METHODIST CHURCH
ATTITUDES ARE
CONTAGIOUS IS YOURS
WORTH CATCHING
SUNDAY SCHOOL 9:45 WORSHIP 11:00
REV. SONNY CHAMPION

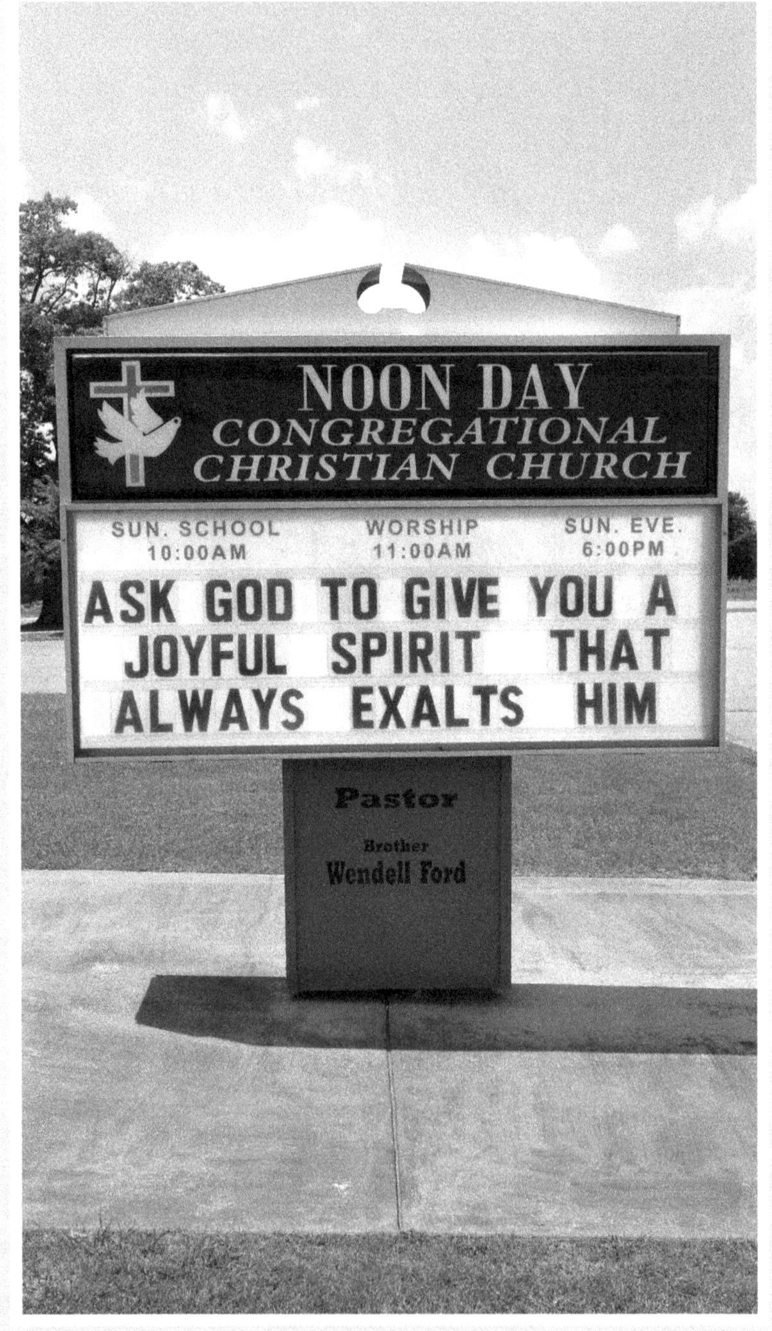
NOON DAY
CONGREGATIONAL
CHRISTIAN CHURCH
SUN. SCHOOL 10:00AM
WORSHIP 11:00AM
SUN. EVE. 6:00PM
ASK GOD TO GIVE YOU A
JOYFUL SPIRIT THAT
ALWAYS EXALTS HIM
Pastor
Brother
Wendell Ford

27

What is the Fruit of the Holy Spirit?

The Holy Spirit living within us should be visible by what grows in us

Galatians 5:22 But the fruit of the Spirit is:

Love,

Joy,

Peace,

Forbearance,

Kindness,

Goodness,

Faithfulness,

Gentleness and

Self-control

Against such things there is no law. 24 Those who belong to Christ Jesus have crucified the flesh with its passions and desires. 25 **Since we live by the Spirit, let us keep in step with the Spirit.** 26 Let us not become conceited, provoking and envying each other.

Dwight
Baptist Church
EST. 1897
MAKE
A
DIFFERENCE
CELEBRATE JESUS

28 What Are the Spiritual Gifts?

We each receive gifts for the common good

1 Corinthians 12:1 Now **about spiritual gifts, brothers and sisters, I
do not want you to be uninformed.** 2 You know that when you were
pagans, somehow or other you were influenced and led astray to mute
idols. 3 Therefore I want you to know that no one who is speaking by
the Spirit of God says, "Jesus be cursed," and no one can say, "Jesus is
Lord," except by the Holy Spirit. 4 **There are different kinds of gifts,
but the same Spirit distributes them.** 5 There are different kinds of
service, but the same Lord. 6 There are different kinds of working, but
in all of them and in everyone it is the same God at work. 7 Now to each
one the manifestation of the Spirit is **given for the common good.** 8 To
one there is given through the Spirit the message of **wisdom,** to another
the message of **knowledge** by means of the same Spirit, 9 to another
faith by the same Spirit, to another gifts of healing by that one Spirit,
10 to another **miraculous powers,** to another **prophecy,** to another **distinguishing between spirits,** to another speaking in **different kinds of
tongues,** and to still another the **interpretation of tongues.** 11 All these
are the work of one and the same Spirit, and he distributes them to each
one, just as he determines.

Seek to excel in gifts that build up the Church

1 Corinthians 14:1 Follow the way of love and **eagerly desire spiritual gifts**, especially prophecy.

1 Corinthians 14:12 So it is with you. Since you are eager to have spiritual gifts, try to **excel in gifts that build up the church.**

1 Corinthians 14:26 What then shall we say, brothers and sisters? When you come together, each of you has a hymn, or a word of instruction, a revelation, a tongue or an interpretation. **Everything must be done so that the church may be built up.** [27] If anyone speaks in a tongue, two—or at the most three—should speak, one at a time, and someone must interpret. [28] If there is no interpreter, the speaker should keep quiet in the church and speak to himself and God.

Understand we do not all have the same gifts

Romans [12:3] For by the grace given me I say to every one of you: Do not think of yourself more highly than you ought, but rather think of yourself with sober judgment, in accordance with the measure of faith God has distributed to each of you. [4] Just as each of us has one body with many members, and these members do not all have the same function, [5] so in Christ we though many, form one body, and each member belongs to all the others. [6] **We have different gifts, according to the grace given us.** If your gift is **prophesying**, then prophesy in accordance with your faith. [7] If it is **serving**, then serve; if it is **teaching**, then teach; [8] if it is **encouraging**, then give encouragement; if it is **giving**, then give generously; if it is to **lead,** do it diligently; if it is to **show mercy**, do it cheerfully.

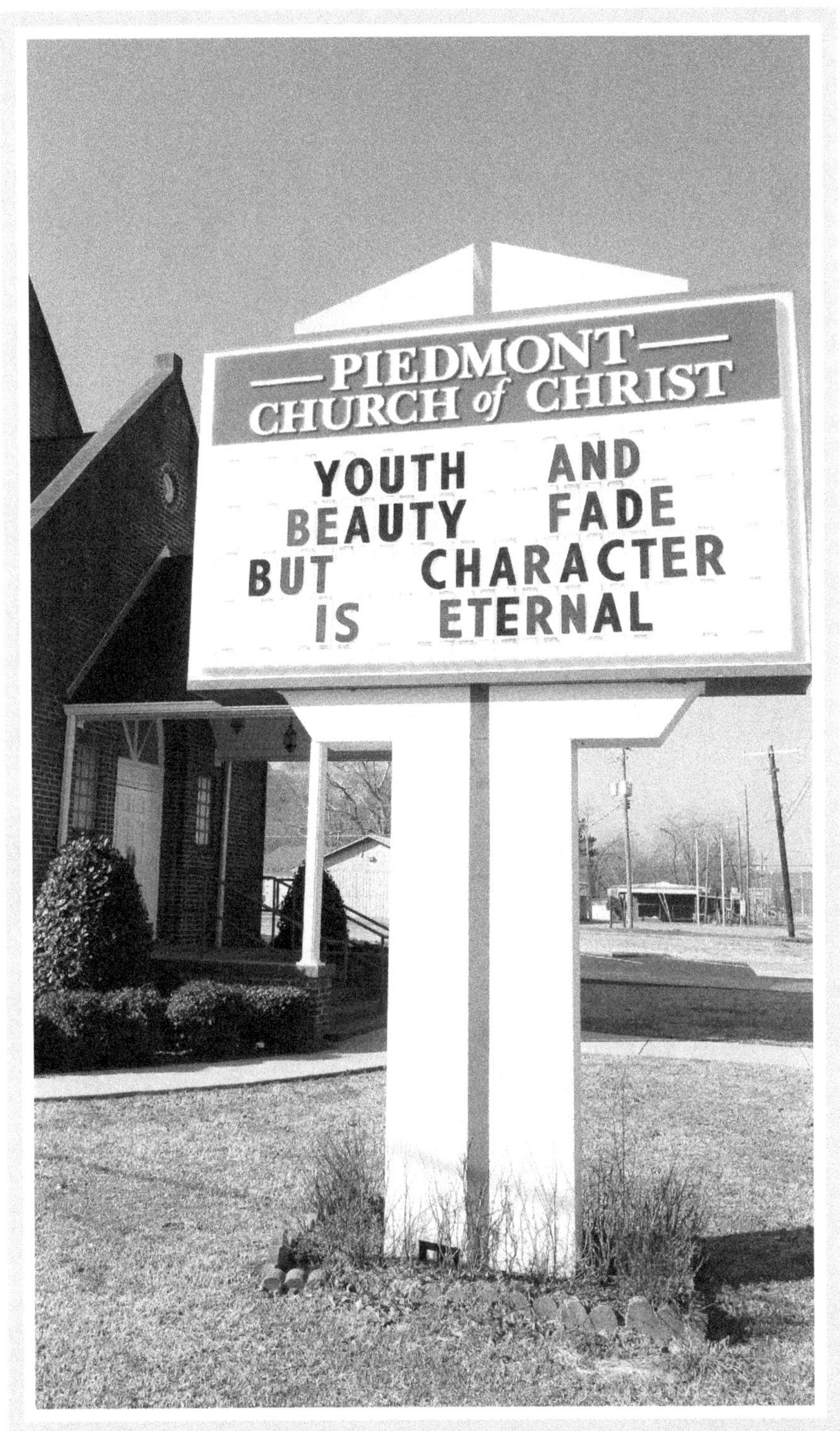
PIEDMONT
CHURCH of CHRIST
YOUTH AND
BEAUTY FADE
BUT CHARACTER
IS ETERNAL

HARMONY
BAPTIST CHURCH
FOR GOD
SO LOVED
HE GAVE
Sunday School 8:45 • Morning Worship 10:00 • Evening Worship 6:00
Wednesday 6:00 PASTOR: Rev. David Jones

29 What Does the Bible Say about Love?

The wise ponder the abounding love of the Lord

Psalm 107:43 **Let the one who is wise** heed these things **and ponder the loving deeds of the LORD.**

Psalm 86:5 You, LORD, are forgiving and good, **abounding in love to all who call to you.**

God Himself told us of His love

Exodus 34: 5 Then the LORD came down in the cloud and stood there with him and proclaimed his name, the LORD. 6 And he passed in front of Moses, proclaiming, **"The LORD, the LORD, the compassionate and gracious God, slow to anger, abounding in love and faithfulness, 7 maintaining love to thousands, and forgiving wickedness, rebellion and sin.** Yet he does not leave the guilty unpunished; he punishes the children and their children for the sin of the parents to the third and fourth generation."

Love is most important

Galatians 5:6 For in Christ Jesus neither circumcision nor uncircumcision has any value. **The only thing that counts is faith expressing itself through love.**

God's love is great

1 John 3:1 **See what great love the Father has lavished on us, that we should be called children of God!** And that is what we are!

Psalm 130:7 Israel put your hope in the LORD, for **with the LORD is unfailing love and with him is full redemption.**

Romans [5:6] You see, at just the right time, when we were still powerless, Christ died for the ungodly. [7] Very rarely will anyone die for a righteous person, though for a good person someone might possibly dare to die. **[8] But God demonstrates his own love for us in this: While we were still sinners, Christ died for us.**

We should love the Lord

Deuteronomy [6:4] Hear, O Israel: The LORD our God, the LORD is one. **[5] Love the LORD your God with all your heart and with all your soul and with all your strength.**

Matthew [22:37] Jesus replied: "**'Love the Lord your God with all your heart and with all your soul and with all your mind.' [38] This is the first and greatest commandment.**

The Lord's love is everlasting

1 Chronicles [16:34] Give thanks to the LORD, for he is good; **his love endures forever.**

Psalm [103:17] But **from everlasting to everlasting the LORD's love is with those who fear him,** and his righteousness with their children's children—

The Lord's love never fails

Psalm [32:10] Many are the woes of the wicked, but **the LORD's unfailing love surrounds the one who trusts in him.**

Psalm [33:5] The LORD loves righteousness and justice; **the earth is full of his unfailing love.**

Psalm [36:5] **Your love, LORD, reaches to the heavens, your faithfulness to the skies.**

Psalm [26:2] Test me, LORD, and try me, examine my heart and my mind; [3] for **I have always been mindful of your unfailing love and have lived in reliance on your faithfulness**

Psalm 33:5 The LORD loves righteousness and justice; **the earth is full of his unfailing love.**

The strength of God's love surpasses all

Romans 8:38 For I am convinced that **neither death nor life, neither**
angels nor demons, neither the present nor the future, nor any pow-
ers, 39 **neither height nor depth, nor anything else in all creation,**
will be able to separate us from the love of God that is in Christ
Jesus our Lord.

Paul tells the Corinthians about love—*this is known as the 'Love Chapter' of the Bible*

1 Corinthians 13:1 If I speak in the tongues of men and of angels, but
have not love, I am only a resounding gong or a clanging cymbal. 2 If I
have the gift of prophecy and can fathom all mysteries and all knowledge, and if I have a faith that can move mountains, but do not have
love, I am nothing. 3 If I give all I possess to the poor and give over my
body to hardship that I may boast, but have not love, I gain nothing.
4 **Love is patient, love is kind. It does not envy, it does not boast, it**
is not proud. 5 **It does not dishonor others, it is not self-seeking, it**
is not easily angered, it keeps no record of wrongs. 6 **Love does not**
delight in evil but rejoices with the truth. 7 **It always protects, always**
trusts, always hopes, always perseveres. 8 **Love never fails.** But where
there are prophecies, they will cease; where there are tongues, they will
be stilled; where there is knowledge, it will pass away. 9 For we know in
part and we prophesy in part, 10 but when completion comes, what is
in part disappears. 11 When I was a child, I talked like a child, I thought
like a child, I reasoned like a child. When I became a man, I put the
ways of childhood behind me. 12 For now we see but only a reflection
as in a mirror; then we shall see face to face. Now I know in part; then
I shall know fully, even as I am fully known. 13 **And now these three**
remain: faith, hope and love. But the greatest of these is love.

Our love for one another makes God's love for us complete

1 John [4:7] Dear friends, let us love one another, for love comes from God. Everyone who loves has been born of God and knows God. [8] **Whoever does not love does not know God, because God is love.** [9] This is how God showed his love among us: He sent his one and only Son into the world that we might live through him. [10] This is love: not that we loved God, but that he loved us and sent his Son as an atoning sacrifice for our sins. [11] Dear friends**, since God so loved us, we also ought to love one another.** [12] **No one has ever seen God; but if we love one another, God lives in us and his love is made complete in us.**

BETHEL MISSIONARY
BAPTIST CHURCH
SUNDAY SCHOOL 9:45
WEDNESDAY MEETING 5:00
MORNING WORSHIP 11:00
SUNDAY EVENING 6:00
LET NO MAN PULL
YOU SO LOW AS TO
HATE HIM. MLK

NEW BETHEL
BAPTIST CHURCH
LIFE IS LIKE A COIN
YOU CAN SPEND IT
AS YOU WISH
BUT ONLY ONCE
Sunday School
10:00 am
Sunday
Morning Worship
11:00 am
Evening Worship
5:30 pm
Wednesday
Bible Study
5:30 pm
Pastor:

30 Should we Tithe?

Definition

Tithe: *to pay or give a tenth part of one's income or produce especially for the support of the church*

Do not steal from God

Malachi [3:8] Will a mere mortal rob God? Yet you rob me. But you ask, "How are we robbing you?" In tithes and offerings. [9] You are under a curse—your whole nation— because you are robbing me. **[10] Bring the whole tithe into the storehouse, that there may be food in my house.**

A challenge from God

Malachi [3:10] **"Test me in this,"** says the LORD Almighty, "and **see if I will not throw open the floodgates of heaven and pour out so much blessing that there will not be room enough to store it.** [11] I will prevent pests from devouring your crops, and the vines in your fields will not drop their fruit before it is ripe," says the LORD Almighty. [12] "Then all the nations will call you blessed, for yours will be a delightful land," says the LORD Almighty.

Give with joy!

2 Corinthians [9:6] Remember this: Whoever sows sparingly will also reap sparingly, and whoever sows generously will also reap generously. **[7] Each of you should give what you have decided in your heart to give, not reluctantly or under compulsion, for God loves a cheerful giver.** [8] And God is able to bless you abundantly, so that in all things at all times, having all that you need, you will abound in every good work.

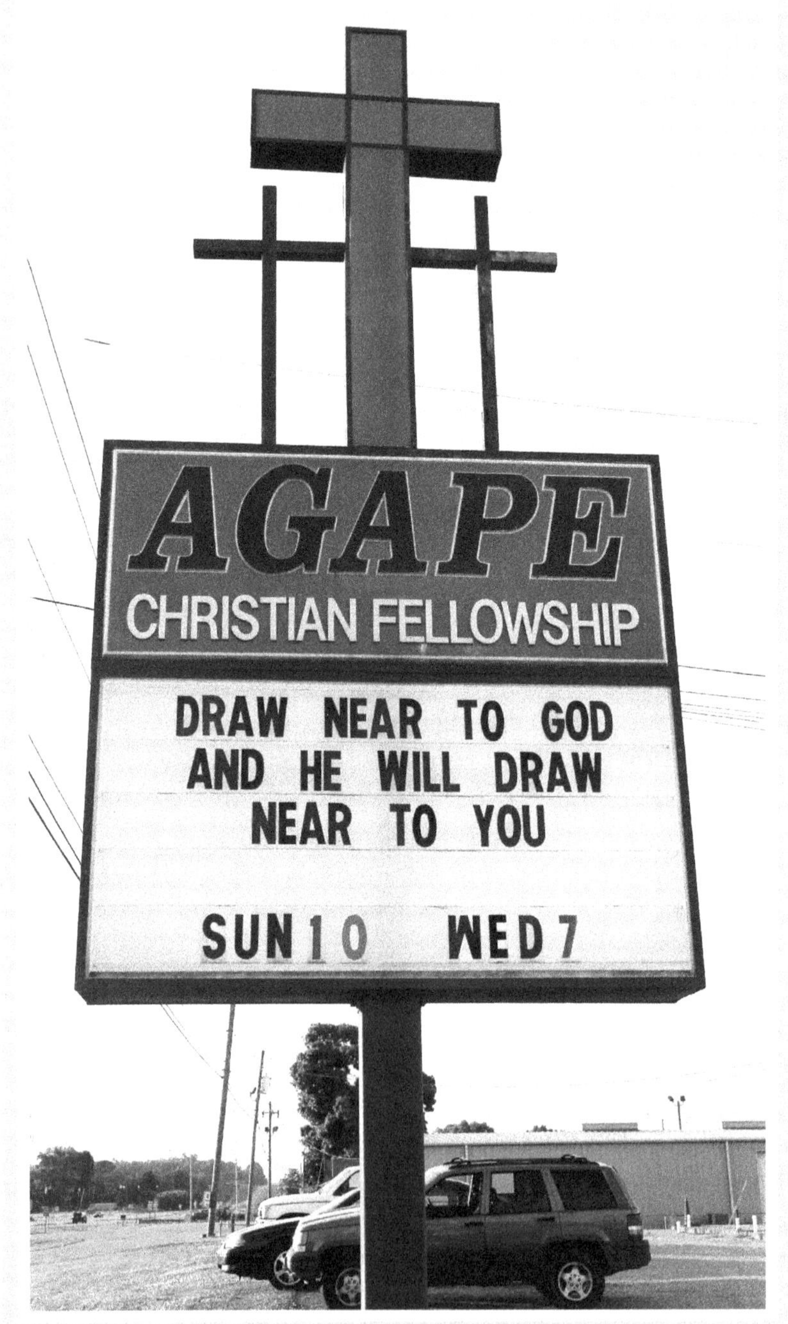
AGAPE
CHRISTIAN FELLOWSHIP
DRAW NEAR TO GOD
AND HE WILL DRAW
NEAR TO YOU
SUN 10 WED 7

31 How should we look at life?

Life has its seasons

Ecclesiastes 3:1 There is a time for everything, and a season for every activity under heaven:

2 a time to be born and a time to die, a time to plant and a time to uproot,

3 a time to kill and a time to heal, a time to tear down and a time to build,

4 a time to weep and a time to laugh, a time to mourn and a time to dance,

5 a time to scatter stones and a time to gather them, a time to embrace and a time to refrain from embracing,

6 a time to search and a time to give up, a time to keep and a time to throw away,

7 a time to tear and a time to mend, a time to be silent and a time to speak,

8 a time to love and a time to hate, a time for war and a time for peace.

Our time on earth is limited and our lives are not long remembered

Psalm 103:15 **The life of mortals is like grass, they flourish like a flower of the field;** 16 the wind blows over it and it is gone, and its place remembers it no more.

King Solomon's conclusion on the matter — Our whole duty

Ecclesiastes [9:10] **Whatever your hand finds to do, do it with all your might**, for in the realm of the dead, where you are going, there is neither working nor planning nor knowledge nor wisdom.

Ecclesiastes [12:13] Now all has been heard; **here is the conclusion of the matter: Fear God and keep his commandments, for this is the duty of all mankind.** [14]

For God will bring every deed into judgment, including every hidden thing, whether it is good or evil.

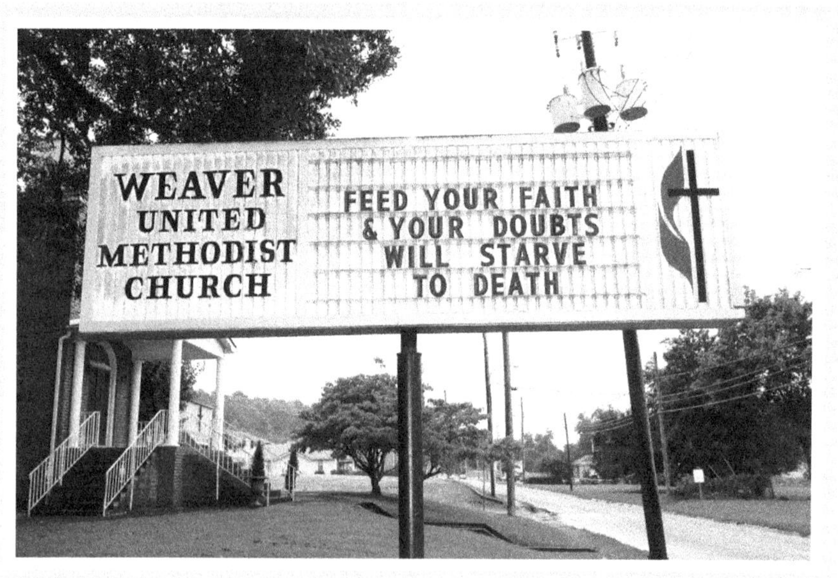

PIEDMONT
CHURCH of CHRIST
LIFE IS A ONE
TIME OFFER
USE IT
WELL

Open Door
Baptist Church
THE DEVIL
WEARS CAMOFLAUGE
Pastor:
Terry Holder
Sunday School 10:00AM
Worship Service 11:00AM
Sunday Night 5:00PM
Wednesday Night 6:30PM

32 How can I know if someone is a Christian?

It is important to know the hearts of those around you. All you need do is ask: Are you a Christian? Then listen to what is said

1 John [4:1] Dear friends, do not believe every spirit, but **test the spirits to see whether they are from God**, because many false prophets have gone out into the world. [2] This is how you can recognize the Spirit of God: **Every spirit that acknowledges that Jesus Christ has come in the flesh is from God,** [3] but every spirit that does not acknowledge Jesus is not from God. This is the spirit of the antichrist, which you have heard is coming and even now is already in the world.

1 Thessalonians [5:19] Do not quench the Spirit's fire; [20] do not treat prophecies with contempt [21] **but test them all; hold on to good.** [22] Reject every kind of evil.

Asberry
BAPTIST CHURCH
HAVE YOU PRAYED ABOUT
IT AS MUCH AS YOU
HAVE TALKED ABOUT IT?
SUNDAY SCHOOL
10:00 AM
WORSHIP
11:00 AM & 6:00 PM
WEDNESDAY
6:30 PM

33 Are Angels Real?

Angels were present before the creation of the world

Job [38:1] Then the LORD spoke to Job out of the storm. He said: [2] "Who is this that obscures my plans with words without knowledge? [3] Brace yourself like a man; I will question you, and you shall answer me. [4] **Where were you when I laid the earth's foundation?** Tell me, if you understand. [5] Who marked off its dimensions? Surely you know! Who stretched a measuring line across it? [6] On what were its footings set, or who laid its cornerstone— [7] **while the morning stars sang together and all the angels shouted for joy?"**

Angels brought death to the Egyptians

Psalm [78:49] He unleashed against them his hot anger, his wrath, indignation and hostility— **a band of destroying angels.** [50] He prepared a path for his anger; he did not spare them from death but gave them over to the plague. [51] He **struck down all the firstborn of Egypt**, the first fruits of manhood in the tents of Ham.

Angels can also be our guardians

Psalm [34:7] The angel of the LORD **encamps around those who fear him, and he delivers them.**

Psalm [91:11] For he **will command his angels concerning you to guard you** in all your ways;

Daniel [6:21] **Daniel answered**, "May the king live forever! [22] **My God sent his angel, and he shut the mouths of the lions.** They have not hurt me, because I was found innocent in his sight. Nor have I ever done any wrong before you, Your Majesty."

Angels are servants of God

Psalm [103:20] Praise the LORD, **you his angels, you mighty ones who do his bidding**, who obey his word.

***Bidding**: an authoritative direction or instruction to do something*

In the endtimes, angels will destroy all who cause sin and do evil

Matthew [13:40] As the weeds are pulled up and burned in the fire, so it will be at the end of the age. [41] The Son of Man will send out **his angels, and they will weed out of his kingdom everything that causes sin and all who do evil.** [42] They will throw them into the blazing furnace, where there will be weeping and gnashing of teeth. [43] Then the righteous will shine like the sun in the kingdom of their Father. Whoever has ears, let them hear.

Angels rejoice when sinners repent

Luke [15:8] Or suppose a woman has ten silver coins and loses one. Doesn't she light a lamp, sweep the house and search carefully until she finds it? [9] And when she finds it, she calls her friends and neighbors together and says, "Rejoice with me; I have found my lost coin." [10] In the same way, **I tell you, there is rejoicing in the presence of the angels of God over one sinner who repents.**

Angels are the escort to the afterlife

Luke [16:22] The time came when **the beggar died and the angels carried him to Abraham's side.** The rich man also died and was buried. In Hades, where he was in torment, he looked up and saw Abraham far away, with Lazarus by his side. [24] So he called to him, "Father Abraham, have pity on me and send Lazarus to dip the tip of his finger in water and cool my tongue, because I am in agony in this fire."

Angels do not die

Luke [20:34] Jesus replied, "The people of this age marry and are given in marriage. [35] But those who are considered worthy of taking part in that age and in the resurrection from the dead will neither marry nor be given in marriage, [36] **and they can no longer die; for they are like the angels. They are God's children, since they are children of the resurrection."**

Angels may masquerade as people

Hebrews [13:1] Keep on loving each other as brothers and sisters. [2] Do not forget to **show hospitality to strangers, for by so doing some people have shown hospitality to angels without knowing it.** [3] Continue to remember those in prison as if you were together with them in prison, and those who are mistreated as if you yourselves were suffering.

Over one-hundred-million angels

Revelation [5:11] Then I looked and heard the voice of many angels, **numbering** thousands upon thousands, and **ten thousand times ten thousand.** They encircled the throne and the living creatures and the elders. [12] In a loud voice they were saying: "Worthy is the Lamb, who was slain, to receive power and wealth and wisdom and strength and honor and glory and praise!"

NEW BETHEL
BAPTIST CHURCH
FOR EVERY
GOLIATH THERE
IS A STONE
Sunday School
10:00 am
Sunday
Morning Worship
11:00 am
Evening Worship
5:30 pm
Wednesday
Bible Study
5:30 pm
Pastor:

34 Can I make it as a Christian?

We will grow tired and we may stumble

Isaiah 40:30 Even youths grow tired and weary, and young men stumble and fall; 31 but **those who hope in the LORD will renew their strength. They will soar on wings like eagles; they will run and not grow weary, they will walk and not be faint.**

Paul, fully understanding the power of God, summed it up

Romans 8:31 What, then, shall we say in response to these things? **If God is for us, who can be against us?**

Romans 8:37 No, in all these things **we are more than conquerors through him who loved us.** 38 For I am convinced that **neither death nor life, neither angels nor demons, neither the present nor the future, nor any powers,** 39 **neither height nor depth, nor anything else in all creation, will be able to separate us from the love of God that is in Christ Jesus our Lord.**

We are promised no temptation is too great to overcome

1 Corinthians 10: 12 So, if you think you are standing firm, be careful that you don't fall! 13 No temptation has overtaken you except what is common to mankind. And **God is faithful; he will not let you be tempted beyond what you can bear. But when you are tempted, he will also provide a way out so that you can endure it.**

STEMLEY BAPTIST CHURCH
MAKE HEAVEN
YOUR
FINISH LINE
SUNDAY WORSHIP SERVICES
11:00 AM & 6:00 PM
REV. CARL ARMSTRONG
WEDNESDAY SERVICE
7:00 PM

35 So How Should I Live My Life?

Offer yourself to God

Romans [6:13] **Do not offer any part of yourself to sin as an instrument of wickedness, but rather offer yourselves to God** as those who have been brought from death to life; and **offer every part of yourself to him as an instrument of righteousness.** [14] For sin shall no longer be your master, because you are not under law, but under grace.

Romans [12:1] **Therefore**, I urge you, brothers and sisters, in view of God's mercy, **to offer your bodies as living sacrifices, holy and pleasing to God—this is your true and proper worship.** [2] **Do not conform to the pattern of this world, but be transformed by the renewing of your mind.** Then you will be able to test and approve what God's will is—his good, pleasing and perfect will.

Do not repay evil for evil

Romans [12:17] Do not repay anyone evil for evil. **Be careful to do what is right in the eyes of everyone.** [18] If it is possible, as far as it depends on you, **live at peace with everyone.** [19] **Do not take revenge, my dear friends, but leave room for God's wrath,** for it is written: "It is mine to avenge; I will repay," says the Lord. [20] On the contrary: **"If your enemy is hungry, feed him; if he is thirsty, give him something to drink. In doing this, you will heap burning coals on his head."** [21] Do not be overcome by evil, but **overcome evil with good**."

Clothe yourself with Jesus

Romans [13: 14] Rather, **clothe yourselves with the Lord Jesus Christ**, and do not think about how to gratify the desires of the flesh.

Know that your body is a temple

1 Corinthians [6:18] Flee from sexual immorality. All other sins a person commits are outside the body, but whoever sins sexually, sins against their own body. [19] Do you not know that **your bodies are a temple of the Holy Spirit,** who is in you, whom you have received from God? You are not your own; [20] you were bought at a price. Therefore **honor God with your body.**

Do not be partners with unbelievers

2 Corinthians [6:14] **Do not be yoked together with unbelievers.** For what do righteousness and wickedness have in common? Or what fellowship can light have with darkness? [15] What harmony is there between Christ and Belial? Or what does a believer have in common with an unbeliever? [16] What agreement is there between the temple of God and idols? For we are the temple of the living God. As God has said: "I will live with them and walk among them, and I will be their God, and they will be my people."

2 Corinthians [6:17] **Therefore, "Come out from them and be separate, says the Lord**. Touch no unclean thing, and I will receive you." [18] **And "I will be a Father to you, and you will be my sons and daughters," says the Lord Almighty."** [7:1] Therefore, since we have these promises, dear friends, let us purify ourselves from everything that contaminates body and spirit, perfecting holiness out of reverence for God.

Ephesians [5:3] But among **you there must not be even a hint of sexual immorality, or of any kind of impurity, or of greed, because these are improper for God's holy people.** [4] Nor should there be obscenity, foolish talk or coarse joking, which are out of place, but rather thanksgiving. [5] For of this you can be sure: No immoral, impure or greedy person—such a person is an idolater—has any inheritance in the kingdom of Christ and of God. [6] Let no one deceive you with empty words, for because of such things God's wrath comes on those who are disobedient. [7] **Therefore do not be partners with them.**

Live as children of light

Ephesians 5:8 For you were once darkness, but now you are light in the Lord. **Live as children of light** 9 (for the fruit of the light consists in all goodness, righteousness and truth) 10 and find out what pleases the Lord. 11 **Have nothing to do with the fruitless deeds of darkness,** but rather expose them. 12 For it is shameful even to mention what the disobedient do in secret.

Settle disputes outside of court

Matthew 5:25 **"Settle matters quickly with your adversary who is taking you to court. Do it while you are still on the way,** or your adversary may hand you over to the judge, and the judge may hand you over to the officer, and you may be thrown into prison."

Paul wrote of lawsuits

1 Corinthians 6:1 If any of you has a dispute with another, do you dare take it before the ungodly for judgment instead of before the LORD's people? 2 Or do you not know that the LORD's people will judge the world? And if you are to judge the world, are you not competent to judge trivial cases? 3 Do you not know that we will judge angels? How much more the things of this life! 4 Therefore, if you have disputes about such matters, do you ask for a ruling from those whose way of life is scorned in the church? 5 I say this to shame you. Is it possible that there is nobody among you wise enough to judge a dispute between believers? 6 But instead, one brother takes another to court—and this in front of unbelievers! 7 **The very fact that you have lawsuits among you means you have been completely defeated already.** Why not rather be wronged? Why not rather be cheated? 8 Instead, you yourselves cheat and do wrong, and you do this to your brothers and sisters.

Work to please the Holy Spirit within you

Galatians 6:7 Do not be deceived: God cannot be mocked. A man reaps what he sows. 8 Whoever sows to please their flesh, from their flesh will reap destruction; **whoever sows to please the Spirit, from the Spirit**

will reap eternal life. [9] Let us not become weary in doing good, for at the proper time we will reap a harvest if we do not give up. [10] Therefore, as we have opportunity, let us **do good to all people, especially to those who belong to the family of believers.**

Our work has been prepared for Us

Ephesians [2:8] For it is by grace you have been saved, through faith—and this not from yourselves, it is the gift of God— [9] not by works, so that no one can boast. [10] For **we are God's handiwork, created in Christ Jesus to do good works, which God prepared in advance for us to do.**

Do not give the devil a foothold

Ephesians [4:25] Therefore each of you must put off falsehood and speak truthfully to your neighbor, for we are all members of one body. [26] **"In your anger do not sin:" Do not let the sun go down while you are still angry,** [27] **and do not give the devil a foothold.**

Wear the full armor of God

Ephesians [6:10] Finally, **be strong in the Lord and in his mighty power.** [11] **Put on the full armor of God** so that you can take your stand against the devil's schemes. [12] For our struggle is not against flesh and blood, but against the rulers, against the authorities, against the powers of this dark world and against the spiritual forces of evil in the heavenly realms. [13] Therefore put on the full armor of God, so that when the day of evil comes, you may be able to stand your ground, and after you have done everything, to stand. [14] Stand firm then, with **the belt of truth** buckled around your waist, with **the breastplate of righteousness** in place, [15] and with your feet fitted with the readiness that comes from **the gospel of peace.** [16] In addition to all this, take up **the shield of faith,** with which you can extinguish all the flaming arrows of the evil one. [17] Take **the helmet of salvation** and **the sword of the Spirit, which is the word of God.** [18] And pray in the Spirit on all occasions with all kinds of prayers and requests. With this in mind, be alert and always keep on praying for all the LORD's people.

Be holy in all you do

1 Thessalonians 4:3 It is God's will that you should be sanctified: that you should avoid sexual immorality; 4 that **each of you should learn to control your own body in a way that is holy and honorable**, 5 not in passionate lust like the pagans, who do not know God; 6 and that in this matter no one should wrong or take advantage of a brother or a sister. The Lord will punish all those who commit such sins, as we told you and warned you before. 7 For **God did not call us to be impure, but to live a holy life.** 8 Therefore, he who rejects this instruction does not reject a human being but God, who gives you his Holy Spirit.

1 Peter 1:13 Therefore, **with minds that are alert and fully sober, set your hope on the grace to be brought to you when Jesus Christ is revealed at his coming.** 14 **As obedient children, do not conform to the evil desires you had when you lived in ignorance.** 15 **But just as he who called you is holy, so be holy in all you do**; 16 for it is written: **"Be holy, because I am holy."**

Train yourself

1 Timothy 4:7 Have nothing to do with godless myths and old wives' tales; rather, **train yourself to be godly.** 8 For physical training is of some value, but godliness has value for all things, **holding promise for both the present life and the life to come.**

Grasp your eternal life

1 Timothy 6:11 But you, man of God, flee from all this, **and pursue righteousness, godliness, faith, love, endurance and gentleness.** 12 **Fight the good fight of the faith. Take hold of the eternal life to which you were called when you made your good confession in** the presence of many witnesses.

2 Timothy 2:15 Do your best to **present yourself to God as one approved**, a worker who does not need to be ashamed and who correctly handles the word of truth. 16 Avoid godless chatter, because those who indulge in it will become more and more ungodly.

Avoid the ungodly

2 Timothy 2:22 **Flee the evil desires of youth**, and pursue righteousness, faith, love and peace, along with those who call on the Lord out of a pure heart. 23 **Don't have anything to do with foolish and stupid arguments**, because you know they produce quarrels. 24 And **the Lord's servant must not be quarrelsome, but must be kind to everyone**, able to teach, not resentful. 25 Opponents must be gently instructed, in the hope that God will grant them repentance leading them to a knowledge of the truth, 26 and that they will come to their senses and escape from the trap of the devil, who has taken them captive to do his will.

2 Timothy 3:1 But mark this: There will be terrible times **in the last days.** 2 **People will be lovers of themselves, lovers of money, boastful, proud, abusive, disobedient to their parents, ungrateful, unholy,** 3 **without love, unforgiving, slanderous, without self-control, brutal, not lovers of the good,** 4 **treacherous, rash, conceited, lovers of pleasure rather than lovers of God—** 5 having a form of godliness but denying its power. **Have nothing to do with them.**

Persevere

Hebrews 10:22 let us draw near to God with a sincere heart and with the full assurance that faith brings, having our hearts sprinkled to cleanse us from a guilty conscience and having our bodies washed with pure water. 23 Let us **hold unswervingly to the hope we profess**, for he who promised is faithful. 24 And let us consider how we may **spur one another on toward love and good deeds,** 25 **not giving up meeting together**, as some are in the habit of doing, but **encouraging one another—and all the more as you see the Day approaching.**

Hebrews 10:35 So **do not throw away your confidence**; it will be richly rewarded. 36 You need to **persevere so that when you have done the will of God, you will receive what he has promised.**

Fix your eyes upon Jesus

Hebrews 12:1 Therefore, since we are surrounded by such a great cloud of witnesses, let us **throw off everything that hinders and the sin that so**

easily entangles. And let us run with perseverance the race marked out for us, [2] **fixing our eyes on Jesus**, the pioneer and perfecter of faith. For the joy set before him he endured the cross, scorning its shame, and sat down at the right hand of the throne of God. [3] Consider him who endured such opposition from sinners, so that you will not grow weary and lose heart.

Continually praise God

Hebrews [13:15] Through Jesus, therefore, let us **continually offer to God a sacrifice of praise—the fruit of lips that openly profess his name**. [16] And do not forget to do good and to share with others, for with such sacrifices God is pleased.

Do more than just listen

James [1:19] My dear brothers and sisters, take note of this: **Everyone should be quick to listen, slow to speak and slow to become angry**, [20] because human anger does not produce the righteousness that God desires. [21] Therefore, **get rid of all moral filth and the evil that is so prevalent and humbly accept the word planted in you, which can save you.** [22] **Do not merely listen to the word, and so deceive yourselves. Do what it says.** [23] Anyone who listens to the word but does not do what it says is like someone who looks at his face in a mirror [24] and, after looking at himself, goes away and immediately forgets what he looks like. [25] But whoever looks intently into the perfect law that gives freedom, and continues in it, not forgetting what he has heard, but doing it— they will be blessed in what they do.

Take action

James [2:14] What good is it, my brothers and sisters, if someone claims to have faith but has no deeds? Can such faith save him? [15] Suppose a brother or sister is without clothes and daily food. [16] If one of you says to them, "Go in peace; keep warm and well fed," but does nothing about their physical needs, what good is it? [17] In the same way, **faith by itself, if it is not accompanied by action, is dead.**

Get closer to God and He will get closer to you

James 4:7 Submit yourselves, then, to God. Resist the devil, and he will flee from you. 8 **Come near to God and he will come near to you.** Wash your hands, you sinners, and purify your hearts, you double-minded. 9 Grieve, mourn and wail. Change your laughter to mourning and your joy to gloom. 10 **Humble yourselves before the Lord, and he will lift you up.**

Remember who controls your future

James 4:13 Now listen, you who say, "Today or tomorrow we will go to this or that city, spend a year there, carry on business and make money." 14 Why, you do not even know what will happen tomorrow. What is your life? **You are a mist that appears for a little while and then vanishes.** 15 **Instead, you ought to say, "If it is the Lord's will, we will live and do this or that."** 16 As it is, you boast in your arrogant schemes. All such boasting is evil. 17 If anyone, then, knows the good he ought to do and doesn't do it, it is sin for them.

Love one another deeply as you crave pure spiritual milk

1 Peter 1:22 Now that you have purified yourselves by obeying the truth so that you have sincere love for each other**, love one another deeply, from the heart.** 23 For you have been born again, not of perishable seed, but of imperishable, through the living and enduring word of God. 24 For, "All people are like grass, and all their glory is like the flowers of the field; the grass withers and the flowers fall, 25 but the word of the Lord endures forever." And this is the word that was preached to you.

1 Peter 2:1 Therefore, **rid yourselves of all malice and all deceit, hypocrisy, envy, and slander of every kind.** 2 **Like newborn babies, crave pure spiritual milk, so that by it you may grow up in your salvation**, 3 now that you have tasted that the Lord is good.

Abstain from sinful desires

1 Peter 2:11 Dear friends, I urge you, as foreigners and exiles, to **abstain from sinful desires, which war against your soul.** 12 Live such good lives among the pagans that, though they accuse you of doing wrong, they may see your good deeds and glorify God on the day he visits us.

Use your gifts to serve others

1 Peter [4:7] The end of all things is near. Therefore **be alert and of sober mind so that you may pray.** [8] **Above all, love each other deeply, because love covers over a multitude of sins.** [9] **Offer hospitality to one another without grumbling.** [10] Each of you should **use whatever gift you have received to serve others, as faithful stewards of God's grace in its various forms.** [11] If anyone speaks, they should do it as one who speaks the very words of God. If anyone serves, they should do so with the strength God provides, so that in all things God may be praised through Jesus Christ. To him be the glory and the power for ever and ever. Amen.

Place your burdens at God's feet

1 Peter [5:6] Humble yourselves, therefore, under God's mighty hand, that he may lift you up in due time. [7] **Cast all your anxiety on him because he cares for you.** [8] Be alert and of sober mind. Your enemy the devil prowls around like a roaring lion looking for someone to devour. [9] Resist him, standing firm in the faith, because you know that the family of believers throughout the world are undergoing the same kind of sufferings. [10] And the God of all grace, who called you to his eternal glory in Christ, after you have suffered a little while, will himself restore you and make you strong, firm and steadfast. [11] To him be the power forever and ever. Amen.

Add to your faith

2 Peter [1:3] His divine power has given us everything we need for a godly life through our knowledge of him who called us by his own glory and goodness. [4] Through these he has given us his very great and precious promises, so that through them you may participate in the divine nature having escaped the corruption in the world caused by evil desires. [5] For this very reason, **make every effort to add to your faith goodness; and to goodness, knowledge;** [6] **and to knowledge, self-control; and to**

self-control, perseverance; and to perseverance, godliness; [7] **and to godliness, mutual affection; and to mutual affection, love.** [8] **For if you possess these qualities in increasing measure, they will keep you from being ineffective and unproductive in your knowledge of our Lord Jesus Christ.** [9] But whoever does not have them is nearsighted and blind, and forgetting that they have been cleansed from their past sins. [10] Therefore, my brothers and sisters, **make every effort to confirm your calling and election. For if you do these things, you will never stumble,** [11] **and you will receive a rich welcome into the eternal kingdom of our Lord and Savior Jesus Christ.**

Become one who lives forever

1 John [2:15] Do not love the world or anything in the world. If anyone loves the world, love for the Father is not in them. [16] For everything in the world—the lust of the flesh, the lust of his eyes and the pride of life—comes not from the Father but from the world. [17] **The world and its desires pass away, but whoever does the will of God lives forever.**

Continue in Christ

1 John [2:28] And now, dear children, **continue in him, so that when he appears we may be confident and unashamed before him at his coming.**

Build yourself up in faith

Jude [1:20] But you, dear friends, **by building yourselves up in your most holy faith and praying in the Holy Spirit,.** [21] **keep yourselves in God's love as you wait for the mercy of our Lord Jesus Christ to bring you to eternal life.**

Jude [1:22] **Be merciful to those who doubt;** [23] **save others by snatching them from the fire**; to others show mercy, mixed with fear—hating even the clothing stained by corrupted flesh.

Romans [12:9] **Love must be sincere. Hate what is evil; cling to what is good.** [10] Be devoted to one another in brotherly love. Honor one another above yourselves. 11 Never be lacking in zeal, but keep your spiritual fervor, serving the Lord. 12 Be joyful in hope, patient in affliction, faithful in prayer. 13 Share with the Lord's people who are in need. Practice hospitality. 14 Bless those who persecute you; bless and do not curse. 15 Rejoice with those who rejoice; mourn with those who mourn. 16 Live in harmony with one another. Do not be proud, but be willing to associate with people of low position. Do not be conceited.

Philippians 4:4 Rejoice in the Lord always. I will say it again: Rejoice! 5 Let your gentleness be evident to all. The Lord is near. 6 **Do not be anxious about anything, but in everything, by prayer and petition, with thanksgiving, present your requests to God.** 7 And the peace of God, which transcends all understanding, will guard your hearts and your minds in Christ Jesus.

Set your hearts on things above

Colossians 3:1 **Since, then, you have been raised with Christ, set your hearts on things above, where Christ is seated at the right hand of God.** 2 **Set your minds on things above, not on earthly things.** 3 For you died, and your life is now hidden with Christ in God. 4 When Christ, who is your life, appears, then you also will appear with him in glory. 5 **Put to death, therefore, whatever belongs to your earthly nature: sexual immorality, impurity, lust, evil desires and greed, which is idolatry.** 6 Because of these, the wrath of God is coming. 7 You used to walk in these ways, in the life you once lived. 8 **But now you must rid yourselves of all such things as these: anger, rage, malice, slander, and filthy language from your lips.** 9 Do not lie to each other, since you have taken off your old self with its practices 10 and have put on the new self, which is being renewed in knowledge in the image of its Creator. 11 Here there is no Gentile or Jew, circumcised or uncircumcised, barbarian, Scythian, slave or free, but Christ is all, and is in all. 12 **Therefore, as God's chosen people, holy and dearly loved, clothe yourselves with compassion, kindness, humility, gentleness and patience.** 13 Bear with each other and forgive one another if any of you has a grievance against someone. **Forgive as the Lord forgave you.** 14 **And over all these virtues put on love, which binds them all together in perfect unity.** 15 **Let the peace of Christ rule in your hearts,** since as members of one body you were called to peace. And be thankful. [16] **Let the message of Christ dwell among you richly** as you teach and admonish one another with all wisdom, through psalms, hymns and songs from the Spirit singing to God with gratitude in your hearts. [17] And **whatever you do, whether in word or deed, do it all in the name of the Lord Jesus, giving thanks to God the Father through him.**

Be joyful always and pray continually

1 Thessalonians [5:12] Now we ask you, brothers and sisters, to respect those who work hard among you, who care for you in the Lord and who admonish you. [13] Hold them in the highest regard in love because of their work. Live in peace with each other. [14] And we urge you, brothers and sisters, warn those who are idle and disruptive, encourage the disheartened, help the weak, be patient with everyone. [15] Make sure that nobody pays back wrong for wrong, but always strive to do what is good for each other and for everyone else. [16] **Rejoice always,** [17] **pray continually,** [18] **give thanks in all circumstances; for this is God's will for you in Christ Jesus.** [19] Do not quench the Spirit. [20] Do not treat prophecies with contempt [21] but test them all; hold on to what is good, [22] reject every kind of evil.

Obey the laws of the land

Titus [3:1] Remind the people to **be subject to rulers and authorities, to be obedient, to be ready to do whatever is good,** [2] to slander no one, to be peaceable and considerate, and always be gentile towards everyone.

Hebrews [13:17] **Have confidence in your leaders and submit to their authority,** because they keep watch over you as those who must give an account. **Do this so that their work will be a joy, not a burden,** for that would be of no benefit to you.

1 Peter [2:13] **Submit yourselves for the Lord's sake to every human authority:** whether to the emperor, as the supreme authority, [14] or to governors, who are sent by him to punish those who do wrong and to commend those who do right. [15] For it is God's will that by doing good you should silence the ignorant talk of foolish men. [16] Live as free people, but do not use your freedom as a cover-up for evil; live as God's slaves. [17] Show proper respect to everyone: love the family of believers, fear God, honor the emperor.

Encourage one another daily

Hebrews [3:12] See to it, brothers and sisters, that none of you has a sinful, unbelieving heart that turns away from the living God. [13] **But encourage one another daily, as long as it is called "Today," so that none of you may be hardened by sin's deceitfulness.** [14] We have come to share in Christ, if indeed we hold our original conviction firmly to the very end.

Have pure and faultless religion

James [1:26] Those who consider themselves religious and yet do not keep a tight rein on their tongues, deceive themselves, and their religion is worthless. [27] **Religion that God our Father accepts as pure and faultless is this: to look after orphans and widows in their distress and to keep oneself from being polluted by the world.**

Finally, seek to inherit your blessing!

1 Peter [3:8] Finally, all of you, **be like-minded; be sympathetic, love one another, be compassionate and humble.** [9] **Do not repay evil with evil or insult with insult. On the contrary, repay evil with blessing, because to this you were called so that you may inherit a blessing.**

Philippians [4:8] Finally, brothers and sisters, **whatever is true, whatever is noble, whatever is right, whatever is pure, whatever is lovely, whatever is admirable—if anything is excellent or praiseworthy—think about such things.** [9] Whatever you have learned or received or heard from me, or seen in me—put it into practice. And the God of peace will be with you.

THE 23RD PSALM
A PSALM OF DAVID

1 The LORD is my shepherd, I lack nothing.

2 He makes me lie down in green pastures,
he leads me beside quiet waters,

3 he refreshes my soul.
He guides me along the right paths
for his name's sake.

4 Even though I walk
through the darkest valley,
I will fear no evil,
for you are with me;
your rod and your staff,
they comfort me.

5 You prepare a table before me
in the presence of my enemies.
You anoint my head with oil;
my cup overflows.

6 Surely your goodness and love will follow me
all the days of my life,
and I will dwell in the house of the LORD
forever.

BOILING SPRINGS
BAPTIST CHURCH
GOD OWES YOU NOTHING
AND
GIVES YOU EVERYTHING

PSALMS
CH. 128
BLUE MOUNTAIN
BAPTIST CHURCH
PASTOR

AFTERTHOUGHT

THESE DAYS I tell folks I am a "Fannie Mae Foot Soldier" and so it has been for the last six or seven years. My children have grown and gone and I spent most of my time working "from can to can't" servicing and selling foreclosed residential properties for the Federal National Mortgage Association (Fannie Mae) in a seven county region of northeast Alabama. There has not been time for much more. Things changed in my home, and at my church, and I stopped teaching Sunday School several years ago.

Today life spins on.

Together, we all spin around on the Earth's axis as we revolve around the sun. What an incredible set of exact conditions enables continued life on this planet! It has gone on this way for millennia. I suspect, life will continue on far longer than you or I will be around to witness.

Life spins on for me individually. When I was younger, I thought it was three B's which kept me spinning: the bills, babies and burdens. Now, I realize my spinning was (and is) the result from a lack of focus and improper prioritization, which hamper and confuse me.

I have bills for sure; they come each month like the ocean tide. The bills come in and the money goes out. I have somehow found ways to keep most of my creditors happy but not a way to dig out of the financial mess I made; the spinning never stops.

Throughout all this spinning, I have picked up and put aside this book project for the last ten years. I think of it as the single most important thing I have to offer; yet, I have also allowed myself to lose focus and turn away from it many times.

But, I did persist. I received encouragement and advice, and there have been frustrations and disappointments.

Dorsey White, the beloved former pastor of a small Methodist church in Wedowee, gave me the greatest compliment of all who have read my efforts. I gave him an early draft copy at an annual "Third Sunday of May Decoration Day" church homecoming. The church, Union

Hill Methodist, is where my grandmother attended church, and where I have been going those third Sundays of May all my life. Pastor White called on a hot August night to say "I have read through your book cover to cover, and I can find nothing wrong with it."

Pastor White died a few years ago. He was an awesome man of God who preached fire and brimstone, along with grace and forgiveness, as well as any preacher I've ever heard. His "endorsement" of my work kept me pursuing this project as much as anything else.

Another motivator has been the ignorance most folks have of the Bible and Biblical teaching. The best example I can give is a reference of a YouTube video from the September 28th, 2007 Democratic Presidential candidates debate. Near the end of the debate the contenders were asked to name their favorite Bible verse. Judge for yourself how the eight folks wishing to lead the most powerful nation on Earth, including our current President Barack Obama, stumbled and failed to name even one "favorite" verse.

I hope this book will be delivered to all members of the United States Congress. I think the elected officials of our government should be without excuse when it comes to knowledge of our God. I believe this book will be translated into multiple languages including Chinese. Millions of Chinese people hunger to understand God's word.

I believe if we are to survive on this planet, we must join together and embrace God's love. Folks of all religions should live peacefully under the umbrella of love. We should communicate, unite, and fight against the masked faces of evil which terrorize the world today.

In the United States, we must pour out God's love on one another. We should embrace people who have found their way to our country, but we must also educate and teach these folks of the greatness and goodness of our country. This greatness and goodness formed almost two hundred fifty years ago when it was written:

"We hold these truths to be self-evident, that ***all men are created equal, that they are endowed by their Creator with certain unalienable Rights, that among these are Life, Liberty and the pursuit of Happiness.*** *—That to secure these rights, Governments are instituted among Men, deriving their just powers from the consent of the governed."*

And much later, we adopted this as our national motto:

IN GOD WE TRUST

And so it has been. And Good Lord willing, so shall it be.

Now more than ever, this country and this world need to understand our God. I hope this book helps, I hope you help as well; **share God's word and love!**

God is love.

I shall conclude by explaining the photos of church signs found throughout this book. I am an avid church sign reader. I have gained much wisdom from church signs through the years.

My mom was a big time prayer warrior. Her prayers have wrapped a cloak of protection around me that guards me still today; however, my mom was a worrier. It was, I thought, her only true character flaw. She worried about me more than any other matter. It almost drove me crazy.

My mom was a God-fearing woman, and the worry thing bothered me greatly. Then, one day, on a church marquee I read:

WORRY IS ABUSE OF THE IMAGINATION

Yes! That is so true. I could not wait to tell my mom. When we worry, we project a negative outcome on a future event. We might imagine the worst possible outcomes without considering the love and faithfulness and care and compassion our God has for us all!

I was hooked. I cannot pass a church sign without slowing down to read it. My mom's reply to it all was "Just remember, David, put feet to your prayers," and we should. Gosh, I miss her.

I have another personal testimony about church sign wisdom. At the height of my distress over a troubled real estate development, I was in battle with a regional bank. Its special assets manager and an attorney were boxing mom and me into a corner, eventually requiring us to liquidate the development at a huge loss.

The development needed a white knight investor to help us through the matter. I contacted every individual I thought could help us and might benefit by becoming the investor. It was 2007, and the real estate industry along with the financial world were on the verge of the largest bust since the Great Depression. There was no one willing and able to help. I was angry, scared, and seemingly without hope.

For the first time in my life, I fantasized about killing someone. Honestly, it was that bad. I thought about "going postal" on the banker and lawyer and any collateral damage that might occur. We employed an attorney at the time, who said of those on the other side, "I like them, but they are a bunch of blood-sucking SOBs."

My thought was simple. They should die. I would do the world a favor by blowing us all up, right there on the 34th floor of the lawyer's conference room. I'd let the debris fall to the street, and the newspapers would tell the story of the customer they had pushed too far. It was a very dark time in my life. The southern rock group The Driveby Truckers released a song around this time entitled "Sinkhole." It made perfect sense to me.

Then, driving down US Highway 21 to Montgomery for some matter, I saw a sign on a small, country church:

GOD HAS FORGIVEN YOU
NOW CAN YOU FORGIVE OTHERS

Forgive? Are you kidding me? I imagined killing those banker folks. I never once thought about forgiving them. But, as I traveled on down the highway, a real peace came upon me. A peace I had not felt in a very long time. A peace that surpasses all understanding. The peace of God's forgiveness. God has forgiven me and continues to forgive me. It is not deserved. I do not understand it, I only believe it. Yes, I am forgiven, and yes, I can, and will, and did forgive others.

Hallelujah! My life changed. We agreed to liquidate the development. We moved on. Yes, it all hurt, and yes, in a real way, I continue to suffer from the financial loss, but I have forgiven those who were doing their assigned job for the bank.

Rebecca Price is one of the individuals who helped me with the design of this book. She gave me excellent advice including to number the questions, start each question as a new chapter, and to illustrate the book in some manner. I told her of my love of church signs and the wisdom they convey. She suggested church signs might become my illustrations.

So, for the past two years as I drove around on Fannie Mae assignments, I stopped and photographed church signs that spoke to me. It seemed as though I waited forever to take the first photo. I missed many. I thought I was either too busy to stop or I could get the photo next time I passed. The first sign I photograph was not even a church sign. It was a free standing reader board that read:

THE EYES OF THE LORD ARE EVERYWHERE BEHOLDING THE EVIL AND THE GOOD.

And it occurred to me God was watching me, and my time was running out. I stopped, snapped the photo, and went on about my way. One of the last signs I photographed read

GOD GAVE YOU A MESSAGE TO SHARE DO NOT KEEP IT TO YOURSELF

My message. **Delight in the Lord, and He will give you the desires of your heart!**

God is love.

May you live long, love hard, and always seek the word of God as your guide. May Peace and Love be with you always.

David Dethrage

6.7.2015

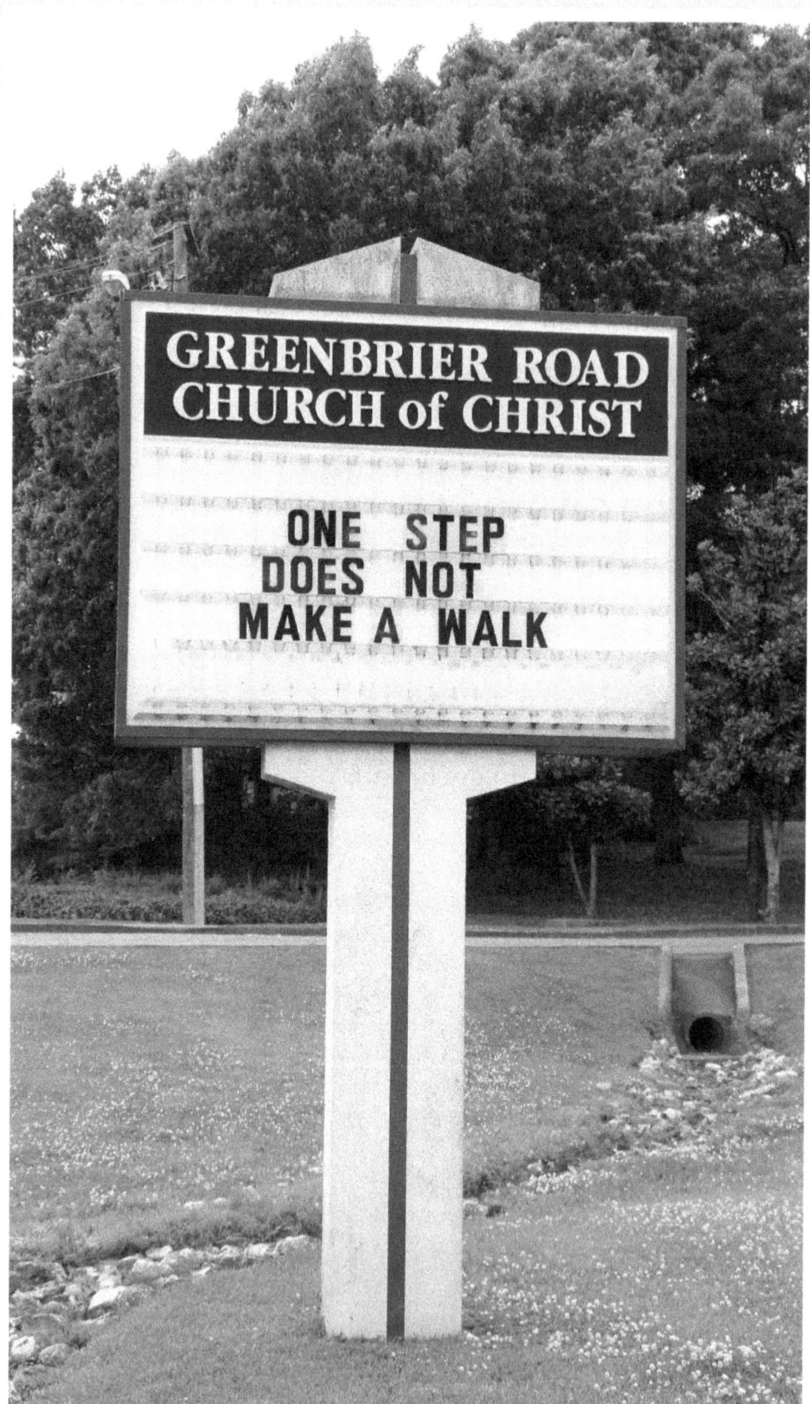
GREENBRIER ROAD
CHURCH of CHRIST
ONE STEP
DOES NOT
MAKE A WALK

Afterthought 2.0

My, my, how God has changed me. My Fannie Mae business went away. Those who worked with me went away. My efforts to promote the first edition of this book failed miserably.

I was confused and dug myself into a deep hole of isolation. I allowed my mind to become consumed with my personal issues and the desires of my flesh.

After a season, I learned I could give this book away with great joy in my heart. Still, I was not able to progress in my efforts to get this book to our government's leadership.

My frustrations compounded my lack of confidence and self-esteem. I dug deeper into my hole.

The events impacting our county including the Pandemic and January 6th Capital Riot further discouraged me.

I allowed my relationship with my wife to deteriorate beyond *my* ability to fix.

Folks, I honestly believe God "disciplined" me. It came as a knockout blow to my ego and as a wrecking ball to all I built my life upon.

Since my junior year at the University of Alabama, I knew what mattered to me most was "family." I knew I wanted to have a glorious family and God Blessed me with the best.

I am ashamed to admit I sailed through most of life's important decisions without seeking God's counsel.

Those who know me well can testify I have always struggled with multiple aspects of my life.

My work, my finances, and my relationships have all suffered tremendously due to my failure to seek God on a daily basis. Still, there was enough "success" for me to hang my hat upon the idea that I was special.

I was as prideful as a man can get concerning my family and my sweet God-sent angel of a wife. Sure, there were aspects which troubled me, but still I knew I was Blessed, and I also knew those troubling aspects were all of my creation.

I felt I was "getting what I deserved" related to the negative issues.

Sadly, I was confident *I* could fix my problems. All my life *I* have tried to fix my problems.

I rarely sought God's guidance for any of them.

I have prayed to and proclaimed God throughout my adult life, yet I failed to seek His guidance on a routine basis.

For the last several years, I was in a severe downward spiral.

I have no doubt I was headed for imminent self-destruction.

On April 27th, my beautiful wife told me she was leaving me.

In the following six days I slept a total of 14 hours and lost 18 pounds.

I spent days and nights wailing as I watched my wife leaving, yet I saw God was revealing Himself to me throughout her departure. I knew what was happening to my marriage was a "God-thing."

At 3:30 a.m. on Monday, May 3rd, I found myself in a horrific state. I had just failed in my attempt to connect with the National Crisis Line before I finally cried out to our Lord.

I pleaded with God to give me *thoughts* that would allow me to move forward with my life. I knew I was incapable of producing those thoughts myself.

Instantly, I was able to find sleep, and things happened immediately.

The first thing which happened was God gave me a giant magnifying glass and told me to take a close look at myself.

When I did, I saw the isolated, sin-filled, prideful, arrogant man I had made of myself.

I saw my lifetime of sin and a lifetime of failing to seek God's guidance on critical issues.

I saw myself swimming alone in a cesspool which was the dark hole of my life resulting from my decades-long withdrawal from friends and family.

I was ashamed, disgusted, and fearful for my life.

God showed me *I* was incapable of fixing myself.

God did not mock me. He did not taunt or tease me, nor did He reject me.

God picked me up, brought me into His loving arms and began to cleanse me.

God cleansed me.

He showed me how my "withdrawal" coping-mechanism had resulted in me living my life mostly alone.

God showed me my failure to *ever* come before Him broken and begging for salvation.

I thought I "had it."

Maybe I did have salvation. I believe I did. God showed me early Monday morning and the following days that I never properly Glorified Him, nor did I apply basic Biblical teaching to my everyday life.

No wonder I sailed my beautiful tall ship (my family) into the rocks just as a category five hurricane hit.

I had spent decades trying to make it through life without God's guidance.

Good Lord willing, all that is over now.

I am a new, different and determined person.

I pray I always remain this way. Every day I ask God to use me as He desires.

My hope is my failures will be a warning to those who will listen.

God is love, and God loves each one of us.

But God is just, and He will not tolerate sin without rebuke.

God commands us to love one another.

If you are not doing so today, *please* begin now to seek God's guidance for your life.

The promises of God are many. His Words are Truth and your life will be Blessed beyond your ability to imagine if you simply . . .

Believe in Christ,

Keep Faith,

Study the Bible, and

Apply His Word to your life!

I also know this . . .

WITH GOD ALL THINGS ARE POSSIBLE.

God Loves us all. God is Glorious.

God's Love never fails!

God has Blessed our nation greatly and He has Blessed me individually.

God wants us all to know . . .

ACTIONS HAVE CONSEQUENCES.

Today, in my eyes, I have lost almost *everything* I worked for and valued.

Except, not really.

I have found God's truth and direction as it relates to my daily life.

I have found new determination to do all as God places upon my heart to accomplish.

I do not know the future, but I know my family is in God's hands.

My hope is by sharing my personal stories you will somehow benefit in a manner which draws you personally closer to God.

Please understand evil is alive and well in our world.

God is Love.

God Loves you, and God Loves US.

May God Bless you; may God Bless US.

May God's Love, our love for Him, and our love for one another fill our great United States of America.

I believe it is our only hope.

David Dethrage

6.7.2021

ROCKFORD
BAPTIST CHURCH
I HAVE A MUSTARD
SEED AND I'M NOT
AFRAID TO USE IT
SUNDAY SCHOOL 10:00
WEDNESDAY MEETING 6:30
MORNING WORSHIP 11:00
SUNDAY EVENING 6:00

ROCKY MT.
BAPTIST
CHURCH

HE WHO KNEELS
BEFORE GOD CAN
STAND BEFORE ANYONE
SUNDAY SCHOOL 9:30AM
WEDNESDAY 10:30AM/6:30PM
MORNING WORSHIP 11:00AM
SUNDAY EVENING 6:00PM
PASTOR: Johnny F. McKinney
1380

Acknowledgments

I am somewhat new to this book writing thing, even though I have been hoping to have this book available in an affordable and desirable format for years.

Once I completed the content text, many years ago, I contacted Jenny Cromnie who previously reported for the *Anniston Star*, to ask if she would help transform my work into an honest-to-goodness book. Jenny was not able to take on the task, but she was kind enough to refer me to Kathy Jennings who became my first editor.

Kathy Jennings is a gracious and patient woman, who helped me understand the importance of standardization of style and accuracy of content. Kathy did great work on my initial draft and gave me a sense of what I hoped my final product would become.

I progressed to the point of believing I was ready for cover design and encountered Rebecca Price through an online search for a professional cover designer. I mentioned Rebecca's contributions earlier and add here she was brutally honest in making me understand this book needed much more work than the draft copy I presented to her.

Time marched on. Rebecca disappeared. I tried to find her, but I have no idea where she went, or even if she is still alive. I do know I am extremely thankful for the significant guidance she provided.

I collected the photographs and placed them within the content and once again sought the help of a graphic design artist to produce the cover. I eventually placed an advertisement on Outsource.com, and met a true God-sent angel. Her name is Francine Eden Platt and her business is Eden Graphics Inc.

Fran agreed to help me with the cover design and in the process I sent her a draft of this book. Wow! My life changed almost overnight. She not only conceived and produced the book cover, she took my work and transformed it into the beautiful contemporary design you see today. Fran became the perfect personification of my design desires. She has worked tirelessly and without complaint about never ending revisions to ensure I was pleased with the outcome. I think she deserves an award for her efforts. What about you?

I wish to thank the fine folks at my primary business, Home Realty Company. Without their work, I would not have been able to maintain my business and income to pursue this project. Terry Wright, the office manager, and Debbie Strickland, Bert and Charlotte Shain, Ed Kelley, Larry Howard and Shaun Winn, who are licensed agents working with me and who have been loyal and supportive without questioning my efforts.

Throughout my trials, frustrations, doubts, and dismay, there has been one constant encourager. I thank you for your unfailing confidence in me.

After a "proof edition" of this book was sent to friends, family, and folks in professional ministry positions, I received excellent critiques and reviews from many. I wish to thank Nancy Turner and Paula Austin for their "English teacher edits," Kathy Jennings, Jeremy Crews, and Phil and Lacey Moon for their extensive critiques, David Haynes, Bob McClain, Al Shackelford, Stan Albright and Alan Medders, each ordained ministers, for their review and encouragement, my family members, Steve Gunnells, Carly Hope, Stephen, and Kathy Jo Dethrage for editing and input, and all the others who took the time to read this work and offer their encouragement.

Finally, I send out thanks to Alison McEmber and Lindsey Leslie at Harper Collins Christian Publishing, and Brett Davis at Biblica for contracting with me to enable the use of NIV Bible scripture. You all have been extremely prompt, professional, and encouraging. Thank you for your continued support.

Second Edition acknowledgments: This book and my efforts to make it beneficial would not have been successful without the continued friendship, support, and encouragement from my book designer, Fran. Erin Gonzales at Harper Collins Christian Publishing allowed me to renew my license for the use of the printed NIV scripture found within *The Desires of Your Heart.* Susan Strauss with Biblica granted worldwide audio and eBook permission for the use of NIV scripture under their "radical generosity" policy. I am confident John Tralka with Heyman Mailing Service, Inc. and Karen Christoffersen of BookWise Publishing are each going to have a HUGE impact on the distribution of this work. **Finally, I know without God all my work is futile. I thank God for his awesome Blessings and His continued work for me.**

Notes

NOTES

Mission Statement

The opposite of love is evil.
God is love.
Christ commanded us to love God and love one another.

Matthew 22: 36–40

My hope is God will use this book and our efforts
to bring the leaders and the people of the United States
together under the banner of love.

That is one tall hope, but I know
With God All Things Are Possible.

Mark 10:27

Contact and Ordering Information

To send comments or if you'd like a FREE electronic copy of this book, please visit our website:

thedesiresofyourheart.com

Printed copies available on Amazon.com

Facebook.com/thedesiresofyourheartbook

CPSIA information can be obtained
at www.ICGtesting.com
Printed in the USA
BVHW052323200721
611781BV00003B/8